Law Made Simple

Powers of Attorney
Simplified

Powers of Attorney
Simplified

by Daniel Sitarz
Attorney-at-Law

Nova Publishing Company
Small Business and Consumer Legal Books and Software
Carbondale, Illinois

ISBN 978-1-892949-40-0
Book w/CD-Rom   price: $24.95

Cataloging-in-Publication

Sitarz, Dan, 1948-
Powers of attorney simplified / by Daniel Sitarz. -- 1st ed. --
    Carbondale, Ill. : Nova Pub. Co., 2007.
    p. ; cm. + 1 CD-ROM.
    (Law made simple)
    ISBN-13: 978-1-892949-40-0
    ISBN-10: 1-892949-40-7
    Includes index.
    1. Power of attorney--United States. 2. Power
    of attorney--United States--Forms. 3. Agency (Law)
    --United States. 4. Agency (Law)--United States--Forms. I. Title.
        KF1347.Z9 S58 2007   346.73/029--dc22 0712

Nova Publishing Company is dedicated to providing up-to-date and accurate legal information to the public. All Nova publications are periodically revised to contain the latest available legal information.

1st Edition; 1st Printing /December 2007

This publication is designed to provide accurate and authoritative information in regard to the subject matter covered. It is sold with the understanding that the publisher and author are not engaged in rendering legal, accounting, or other professional services. If legal advice or other expert assistance is required, the services of a competent professional person should be sought.
—*From a Declaration of Principles jointly adopted by a Committee of the American Bar Association and a Committee of Publishers*

DISCLAIMER

Because of possible unanticipated changes in governing statutes and case law relating to the application of any information contained in this book, the author, publisher, and any and all persons or entities involved in any way in the preparation, publication, sale, or distribution of this book disclaim all responsibility for the legal effects or consequences of any document prepared or action taken in reliance upon information contained in this book. No representations, either express or implied, are made or given regarding the legal consequences of the use of any information contained in this book. Purchasers and persons intending to use this book for the preparation of any legal documents are advised to check specifically on the current applicable laws in any jurisdiction in which they intend the documents to be effective.

Nova Publishing Company
Small Business and Consumer Legal Books and Software
1103 West College St.
Carbondale, IL 62901
Tech Support: (800) 748-1175
Editorial: (618)457-3521

Distributed by:
National Book Network
4501 Forbes Blvd., Suite 200
Lanham, MD 20706
Orders: (800) 462-6420 or
www.novapublishing.com

Nova Publishing Company Green Business Policies

Nova Publishing Company is committed to preserving ancient forests and natural resources. Our company's policy is to print all of our books on recycled paper, with no less than 30% post-consumer waste de-inked in a chlorine-free process. In addition, all Nova books are printed using soy-based inks. As a result, for the printing of this book, we have saved:

10.9 trees • 3,150 gallons of water • 1,845 kilowatt hours of electricity • 27 pounds of pollution

Nova Publishing Company is a member of Green Press Initiative, a nonprofit program dedicated to supporting publishers in their efforts to reduce their use of fiber obtained from endangered forests. For more information, go to www.greenpressinitiative.org. In addition, Nova uses all compact fluorescent lighting; recycles all office paper products, aluminum and plastic beverage containers, and printer cartridges; uses 100% post-consumer fiber, process-chlorine-free, acid-free paper for 95% of in-house paper use; and, when possible, uses electronic equipment that is EPA Energy Star-certified. Finally, all carbon emissions from office energy use are offset by the purchase of wind-energy credits that are used to subsidize the building of wind turbines on the Rosebud Sioux Reservation in South Dakota (see www.nativeenergy.com/coop/).

Table of Contents

LIST OF FORMS
(in book and on CD)

All Forms on CD are in PDF and text format unless noted.

Additional Information for Power of Attorney

Agent's Certification of the Validity of Power of Attorney and Agent's Authority

General Power of Attorney

Unlimited Power of Attorney

Limited Power of Attorney

Limited Power of Attorney for Real Estate

Limited Power of Attorney for Child Care

Durable Unlimited Power of Attorney (effective immediately)

Durable Unlimited Power of Attorney (effective on disability)

Durable Health Care Power of Attorney

Revocation of Durable Health Care Power of Attorney

Witness Affidavit of Revocation of Durable Health Care Power of Attorney

Revocation of Power of Attorney

State-Specific Durable Powers of Attorney (18 forms) (PDF only)

> *Alaska, Arkansas, California, Colorado, Connecticut, District of Columia, Georgia, Illinois, Montana, Nebraska, New Hampshire, New Mexico, New York, North Carolina, Oklahoma, Pennsylvania, Rhode Island, Texas*

Revocation of Advance Health Care Directive

Witness Affidavit of Revocation of Advance Health Care Directive

Additional Information for Advance Health Care Directive

The Following forms are only provided on the CD and only as PDF forms:

Advance Health Care Directives (51 forms)

> *All 50 states and District of Columbia*

CHAPTER 1
How To Use This Book

In each chapter of this book you will find an introductory section that will give you an overview of the types of situations in which the forms in that chapter will generally be used. Following that overview, there will be a brief explanation of the specific uses for each form. Finally, for each form, there is a listing of the information that must be compiled to complete the form. The preferable manner for using these forms is to use the enclosed Forms-on-CD. Instructions for using the Forms-on-CD are included later in this chapter. However, it is perfectly acceptable to prepare these forms directly from the book by making a copy of the form, filling in the information that is necessary, and then retyping the form in its entirety (on your computer) and printing it out on on clean white letter-sized paper.

Before you prepare any of the forms for use, you should carefully read the introductory information and instructions in the chapter where the particular form is contained. Try to be as detailed and specific as possible as you fill in these forms. The more precise the description, the less likelihood that later disputes may develop over what was actually intended by the language chosen. The careful preparation and use of the legal forms in this book should provide you with the proper documents for most power of attorney situations. If in doubt as to whether a particular form will work in a specific application, please consult a competent lawyer.

Installation Instructions for the Forms-on-CD

Quick-Start Installation for PCs
1. Insert the enclosed CD in your computer.
2. The installation program will start automatically. Follow the onscreen dialogue and make your appropriate choices.
3. If the CD installation does not start automatically, click on START, then RUN, then BROWSE, and select your CD drive, and then select the file "Install.exe." Finally, click OK to run the installation program.
4. During the installation program, you will be prompted as to whether or not you wish to install the Adobe Acrobat Reader® program. If you do not already have the Adobe Acrobat Reader® program installed on your hard drive, you will need to select the full installation that will install this program to your computer.

Installation Instructions for MACs®
1. Insert the enclosed CD in your computer.
2. Copy the folder "Forms for Macs" to your hard drive. All of the PDF and text-only forms are included in this folder.

3. If you do not already have the Adobe Acrobat Reader® program installed on your hard drive, you will need to download the version of this software that is appropriate for you particular MAC operating system from www.adobe.com. Note: The latest versions of the MAC operating system (OS-X) has PDF capabilities built into it.

Instructions for Using Forms-on-CD

All of the forms which are included in this book have been provided on the Forms-on-CD for your use if you have access to a computer. If you have completed the Forms-on-CD installation program, all of the forms will have been copied to your computer's hard drive. By default, these files are installed in the C:\Powers of Attorney\Forms folder which is created by the installation program. (Note for MAC users: see instructions above). Opening the Forms folder will provide you with access to folders for each of the topics corresponding to chapters in the book. Within each chapter, the forms are provided in two separate formats:

Text forms which may opened, prepared, and printed from within your own word processing program (such as Microsoft Word®, or WordPerfect®). The text forms all have the file extension: .txt. These forms are located in the TEXT FORMS folders supplied for each chapter's forms. You may wish to use the forms in this format if you will be making changes to text of the forms. To access these forms, please see below.

PDF forms which may be filled in on your computer screen and printed out on any printer. This particular format provides the most widely-used cross-platform format for accessing computer files. Files in this format may be opened as images on your computer and printed out on any printer. The files in PDF format all have the file extension: .pdf. Although this format provides the easiest method for completing the forms, the forms in this format can not be altered (other than to fill in the information required on the blanks provided). To access the PDF forms, please see below. If you wish to alter the language in any of the forms, you will need to access the forms in their text-only versions. To access these text-only forms, please also see below.

To Access PDF Forms

1. You must have already installed the Adobe Acrobat Reader® program to your computer's hard drive. This program is installed automatically by the installation program. (MAC users will need to install this program via www.adobe.com).

2. On your computer's desktop, you will find a shortcut icon labeled "Acrobat Reader®" Using your mouse, left double click on this icon. This will open the Acrobat Reader® program. When the Acrobat Reader® program is opened for the first time, you will need to accept the Licensing Agreement from Adobe in order to use this program. Click "Accept" when given the option to accept or decline the Agreement.

3. Once the Acrobat Reader® program is open on your computer, click on FILE (in the upper left-hand corner of the upper taskbar). Then click on OPEN in the drop down menu. Depending on which version

of Windows or other operating system you are using, a box will open which will allow you to access files on your computer's hard drive. The files for Powers of Attorney are located on your computer's "C" drive, under the folder "Powers of Attorney." In this folder, you will find a subfolder "Forms." (Note: if you installed the forms folder on a different drive, access the forms on that particular drive).

4. If you desire to work with one of the forms, you should then left double-click your mouse on the sub-folder: "Forms." This will open two folders: one for text forms and one for PDF forms. Left double click your mouse on the PDF forms folder and a list of the PDF forms for that topic should appear. Left double click your mouse on the form of your choice. This will open the appropriate form within the Adobe Acrobat Reader® program.

To Fill in Forms in the Adobe Acrobat Reader® Program

1. Once you have opened the appropriate form in the Acrobat Reader® program, filling in the form is a simple process. A 'hand tool' icon will be your cursor in the Acrobat Reader® program. Move the 'hand tool' cursor to the first blank space that will need to be completed on the form. A vertical line or "I-beam" should appear at the beginning of the first space on a form that you will need to fill in. You may then begin to type the necessary information in the space provided. When you have filled in the first blank space, hit the TAB key on your keyboard. This will move the 'hand' cursor to the next space which must be filled in. Please note that some of the spaces in the forms must be completed by hand, specifically the signature, witness, and notary blanks.

2. Move through the form, completing each required space, and hitting TAB to move to the next space to be filled in. For information on the information required for each blank on the forms, please read the instructions in this book. When you have completed all of the fill-ins, you may print out the form on your computer's printer. (Please note: hitting TAB after the last fill-in will return you to the first page of the form.)

3. IMPORTANT NOTE: Unfortunately, the Adobe Acrobat Reader® program does NOT allow you to save the filled-in form to your computer's hard drive. You can only save the form in a printed version. For this reason, you should wait to complete the forms until you have all of the information necessary to complete the chosen form in one session. You may, of course, leave the Acrobat program open on your computer and leave a partially-completed form open in the program. However, if you close the file or if you close the Acrobat Reader® program, the filled-in information will be lost.

To Access and Complete the Text Forms

For your convenience, most of the forms in this book are also provided as text-only forms which may be altered and saved. To open and use any of the text forms:

1. First, open your preferred word processing program. Then click on FILE (in the upper left-hand corner of the upper taskbar). Then click on OPEN in the drop down menu. Depending on which version of Windows or other operating system you are using, a box will open which will allow you to access files on your computer's hard drive. The files for Powers of Attorney are located on

your computer's "C" drive, under the folder "Powers of Attorney." In this folder, you will find a sub-folder: "Forms."

2. If you desire to work with one of the forms, you should then left double-click your mouse on the sub-folder: "Forms." A list of form topics (corresponding to the chapters in the book) will appear and you should then left double-click your mouse on the topic of your choice. This will open two folders: one for text forms and one for PDF forms. Left double click your mouse on the text forms folder and a list of the text forms for that topic should appear. Left double click your mouse on the form of your choice. This will open the appropriate form within your word processing program.

3. You may now fill in the necessary information while the text-only file is open in your word processing program. You may need to adjust margins and/or line endings of the form to fit your particular word processing program. Note that there is an asterisk (*) in every location in these forms where information will need to be included. Replace each asterisk with the necessary information. When the form is complete, you may print out the completed form and you may save the completed form. If you wish to save the completed form, you should rename the form so that your hard drive will retain an unaltered version of the form.

Technical Support

Nova Publishing will provide technical support for installing the provided software. Please also note that Nova Publishing Company cannot provide legal advice regarding the effect or use of the forms on this software. For questions about installing the Forms-on-CD, you may call Nova Technical Support at 1-800-748-1175.

In addition, Nova cannot provide technical support for the use of the Adobe Acrobat Reader®. For any questions relating to Adobe Acrobat Reader®, please access Adobe Technical Support at www.adobe.com/support/main.html or you may search for assistance in the HELP area of Adobe Acrobat Reader® (located in approximately the center of the top line of the program's desktop).

CHAPTER 2
Understanding Powers of Attorney

A power of attorney is simply a document that is used to allow one person to give authority to another person to act on their behalf. The person signing the power of attorney (generally referred to as the *principal*) grants legal authority to another to "stand in their shoes" and act legally for them. The person who receives the such authority is called an *attorney-in-fact*. This title and the power of attorney form *does not* mean that the person receiving the power has to be a lawyer. If you appoint your spouse or a trusted relative or friend, then that person is your "attorney-in-fact". Think of the term "attorney-in-fact" as actually meaning "agent." Using a power of attorney, you will be appointing an "agent" to act in your place for some activities, perhaps relating to financial actions or perhaps relating to health care decisions, or any of a number of other possible actions that your "agent" may perform. The word 'attorney' in the context of a power of attorney or an attorney-in-fact is *not* related to the generally accepted notion of an 'attorney' as a lawyer.

Uses of Powers of Attorney

Power of attorney forms are useful documents for many occasions. They can be used to authorize someone else to sign certain documents if you can not be present when the signatures are necessary. They can be used to authorize someone to handle any or all of the following possible matters:

> Real estate transactions;
> Goods and services transactions;
> Stock, bond, share and commodity transactions;
> Banking transactions;
> Business operating transactions;
> Insurance transactions;
> Estate transactions;
> Legal claims and litigation;
> Personal relationships and affairs;
> Benefits from military service;
> Records, reports and statements;
> Retirement benefit transactions;
> Making gifts to a spouse, children, parents and other descendants;
> Tax matters;
> And, more recently, all personal decisions relating to health care.

Traditionally, banking and real estate matters were the most typical type of actions handled with powers of attorney. Increasingly, however, all manner of affairs are being handled with the prudent use of a power of attorney.

Power of Attorney Definitions

There are many types of power of attorney forms and it is easy to confuse the terminology that is used to describe them. Here are a few definitions to help you understand powers of attorney:

Advance Health Care Directive: A comprehensive form for providing for your health care wishes that generally combines a *living will*, a *durable health care power of attorney*, designation of primary physician, and an organ donation form.

Agent: A person that is appointed in a power of attorney document to act on behalf of another person. Also referred to as an *attorney-in-fact*.

Attorney-in-Fact: A person that is appointed in a power of attorney document to act on behalf of another person. This person *does not* have to be an attorney. Also referred to as an *agent*.

Child Care Power of Attorney: A power of attorney that allows the *principal* to appoint someone to make limited child care decisions regarding a child of the *principal* (generally, limited to providing consent to emergency medical care and/or authority to enroll a child in school).

Durable Power of Attorney: A power of attorney that is not affected by the disability or incapacity of the person that signed it (the *principal*). Note that durable powers of attorney can be of two distinct types: 1) it may take effect immediately and remain in effect *even if* the principal should become incapacitated, or 2) it may *only* take effect if the principal should become incapacitated (this is technically referred to as a *springing power of attorney*).

Financial Power of Attorney: Generally, any power of attorney (other than a *durable health care power of attorney*) that allows the *attorney-in-fact* or *agent* to make financial decisions or take financial action on behalf of the *principal*.

General Power of Attorney: This type of power of attorney allows the *principal* to select among a list of powers and grant the *agent* any or all of the listed powers. If a *principal* wishes to grant unlimited authority to an *agent* however, an *unlimited power of attorney* should be used.

Durable Health Care Power of Attorney: A specialized power of attorney that allows the *principal* to appoint someone (the *attorney-in-fact* or *agent*) to make health care and medical decisions for them if they are unable to communicate their own wishes or decisions to health care providers. This form is intended to take effect only upon the principal's incapacitation.

Limited Power of Attorney: This type of power of attorney is a grant of authority to another person (the *attorney-in-fact* or *agent*) that is limited in scope or duration (for example, to handle a real estate closing on a certain date).

Living Will: A document that allows you to make end-of-life decisions in advance of medical situations that may leave you unable to communicate your wishes regarding the use of artificial life support systems. Often a living will is part of an *advance health care directive*.

Notary: A notary public is a public official whose duty it is to verify signatures on documents. Most banks provide notary services. All power of attorney forms in this book require notarization.

Power of Attorney: A legal document that allows one person (the *principal,* generally, you) to appoint another (the *attorney-in-fact* or *agent*) to act on their behalf.

Principal: The person who authorizes another person to act on their behalf using a power of attorney. Generally, this person is you.

Springing Power of Attorney: A type of durable power of attorney that only takes effect upon the incapacity of the *principal* (it springs into effect on the happening of that event). Can also be prepared (by a lawyer) to take effect on the happening of some other type of event.

Successor Attorney-in-Fact: A person that is appointed in a power of attorney document to act on behalf of another person if the original attorney-in-fact is unable or unwilling to act. This person *does not* have to be an attorney.

Unlimited Power of Attorney: Generally, any power of attorney that allows the *attorney-in-fact* or *agent* to make any and all decisions or take any and all action (except health care decisions and actions) on behalf of the *principal.* The u*nlimited power of attorney* contained in this book is an extremely detailed list of the powers and authority that the *principal* grants to the *agent.* It is intended to cover any and all possible decisions and actions that the *agent* might be called upon to make or perform on behalf of the *principal.*

Types of Powers of Attorney

Let's take a look at the various different types of powers of attorney. (Note that the plural for power of attorney is "powers of attorney" and not "power of attorneys." That is because the legal document is actually creating a "power," the ability for someone else to act on your behalf. The legal document provides them with the "power" to do so.) The following will be a very brief explanation of the types of powers of attorney. Each specific chapter will contain a more detailed description of each type of power of attorney. You should read through this list carefully to determine which type of power of attorney is most appropriate in your particular circumstances. At the end of this chapter, a chart detailing the different types of powers of attorney is provided. Here are the various types of powers of attorney that are included in this book:

General Power of Attorney: Chapter 3 contains a basic power of attorney that allows you to authorize your agent (your "attorney in fact") to handle a few or all of your financial and/or business transactions. With this form, you are giving another person the right to manage some or perhaps all of your financial and/or business matters on your behalf. They are given the power to act exactly as you could. This can be a very powerful grant of authority to someone else to act on your behalf. The person appointed must be someone that you fully trust to handle your affairs. This power of attorney is not valid if you become disabled or incapacitated. You must use a 'durable' power of attorney for that purpose (see below). It also can *not* be used for health care decisions.

Unlimited Power of Attorney: In Chapter 4, you will find a power of attorney that grants your agent (your "attorney in fact") full and complete power to handle all of your business and financial affairs. With this form, you are giving another person the right to manage any and all of your financial and/or business matters on your behalf. They are given the power to act exactly as you could. This particular power of attorney form is very extensive as it lists in great detail all of the powers that your agent (attorney-in-fact) is authorized to exercise. This is an extremely powerful grant of authority to someone else to act on your behalf. The person appointed must be someone that you fully trust to handle your affairs. This power of attorney is not valid if you become disabled or incapacitated. You must use a 'durable' power of attorney for that purpose (see below). It also can *not* be used for health care decisions.

Limited Power of Attorney: Chapter 5 contains a power of attorney that grants your agent (your "attorney in fact") only the exact power to handle the matter that you specifically spell out in the document. The power granted may be limited time-wise (the power to act only on a certain day, for example), geographically (handle financial affairs only in Texas, for example), transactionally (handle only insurance affairs, for example). With this form, you are giving another person the right to handle a particular financial and/or business matter on your behalf. They are given the power to act exactly as you could in the specific situation. This can be is a very powerful grant of authority to someone else to act on your behalf. The person appointed must be someone that you fully trust to handle your affairs. This power of attorney is not valid if you become disabled or incapacitated. You must use a 'durable' power of attorney for that purpose (see below). It also can *not* be used for health care decisions.

Limited Power of Attorney for Real Estate: This power of attorney, also contained in Chapter 5, is a type of limited power of attorney that is specifically written to allow you to grant someone the authority to handle a specific real estate transaction, for example, a real estate closing. With this form, you are giving another person the right to handle a particular financial and/or business matter relating to real estate on your behalf. They are given the power to act exactly as you could in the specific situation. This power of attorney is not valid if you become disabled or incapacitated. You must use a 'durable' power of attorney for that purpose (see below). This form also can *not* be used for health care decisions.

Limited Power of Attorney for Child Care: Also contained in Chapter 5, this power of attorney is a type of limited power of attorney that is specifically written to allow you to grant someone the authority to consent to medical treatment of a minor child, enroll a child in a school, or exercise other child care powers. With this form, you are giving another person the right to handle a particular child care matter on your behalf. They are given the power to act exactly as you could in the specific situation related to child care.

Durable Unlimited Power of Attorney for Financial Affairs (effective immediately): Chapter 6 provides two different durable powers of attorney. The term "durable" means that this type of power of attorney is not affected by your health. In other words, a durable power of attorney remains in effect even if you become disabled and/or incapacitated. A durable unlimited power of attorney for financial affairs allows you to appoint someone to handle your financial affairs during a period that you are unable to handle them yourself. This is a power of attorney that grants your agent (your "attorney in fact") full and complete power to handle all of your business and financial affairs. With this form, you are giving another person the right to manage your financial and/or business matters on your behalf. They are given the power to act exactly as you could. The person appointed must be someone that you fully trust to handle your affairs. This particular durable power of attorney is effective immediately (as opposed to a durable power of attorney that *only* becomes effective upon your disability—see below). This type of power of attorney, however, can *not* be used for health care decisions. You must use a 'durable health care power of attorney' for that purpose. Compare this type of durable power of attorney (that takes effect immediately and remains in effect even if the principal is incapacitated) with the following type of durable power of attorney (that only takes effect upon the principal's incapacity or disability). Please note that this form provides a release for your attorney-in-fact to receive your medical records under the federal HIPAA regulations relating to the privacy of health care records. This does not confer any authority for your attorney-in-fact to make health care decisions on your behalf. The HIPAA release is for the purpose of allowing your attorney-in-fact to have access to your medical files for the purpose of paying or examining medical bills and charges.

Durable Unlimited Power of Attorney for Financial Affairs (effective on disability): Another type of durable power of attorney found in Chapter 6, this is a power of attorney that grants your agent (your "attorney in fact") full and complete power to handle all of your business and financial affairs, but only when and if you become incapacitated and unable to handle your own affairs. The term "durable" means that this type of power of attorney is not affected by your health. In other words, a durable power of attorney, such as this, is valid if you become disabled and/or incapacitated. This power of attorney is effective *only* upon your disability (as opposed to a durable power of attorney that becomes effective immediately and remains in effect regardless of your disability or incapacity—see above). This type of durable power of attorney requires that a physician certify that you are unable to handle your own affairs before your chosen agent (attorney-in-fact) takes control of your financial affairs. A durable unlimited power of attorney for financial affairs allows you to appoint someone to handle your financial affairs during a period that you are unable to handle them yourself. This type of power of attorney, however, can *not* be used for health care decisions. You must use a 'durable health care power of attorney' for that purpose. Please note that this form provides a release for your attorney-in-fact to receive your medical records under the federal HIPAA regulations relating to the privacy of health care records. This does not confer any authority for your attorney-in-fact to make health care decisions on your behalf. The HIPAA release is for the purpose of allowing your attorney-in-fact to have access to your medical files for the purpose of paying or examining medical bills and charges.

Durable Health Care Power of Attorney: Chapter 7 provides a durable health care power of attorney. This is a specialized type of power of attorney that has been developed to allow you to authorize another person to make all of your health care decisions for you in the event that you become disabled or incapacitated and unable to make such decisions for yourself. This is a very powerful document that, in some cases, grants someone else the power of life or death over you. This document allows the person you designate to make health care decisions whenever you are unable to communicate your own desires. As such, it is much more powerful than a living will (which generally provides a statement of your wishes should you be terminally ill or in a persistent vegetative state). Note that this is also a type of "durable" power of attorney in that it is effective even if you incapacitated and are unable to communicate your wishes and desires regarding your health care choices.

State Specific Durable Powers of Attorney: Chapter 9 of this book provides state-specific versions of durable powers of attorney for financial affairs. While the forms provided in Chapter 6 of this book (durable unlimited powers of attorney for financial affairs) are legally-valid in all states, some states provide their own particular form for a durable power of attorney. You may choose to use one of the generic forms provided in Chapter 6 or you may choose to use the state-specific forms provided in Chapter 9. Please check the Appendix for your state listing to determine if your state has a state-specific form for this purpose.

Advance Health Care Directives: These forms are provided only on the CD that is enclosed with this book. An advance health care directive is a legal document that has been developed in most states that incorporates various health care matters into a single comprehensive form. These documents contain the following forms: living will, appointment of health care agent (a health care power of attorney), designation of primary physician, and organ donation. Please see the instructions for advance health care directives in Chapter 10 if you are interested in this type of form.

Revocation of Power of Attorney: Chapter 8 provides a form that may be used to revoke any of the powers of attorney in this book. Chapter 7 contains a revocation specifically tailored to revoke a durable health care power of attorney. In addition, instructions for a revocation of advance health care directive are contained in Chapter 10 and this form is contained on the enclosed CD. Finally, there are two forms that allow for the oral revocation of a durable health care power of attorney or of an advance health care directive. These forms are found, respectively, in Chapters 7 and 10.

Additional Information for Power of Attorney: At the end of this chapter is provided a form that may be used with any of the power of attorney forms in this book (except the durable health care power of attorney. A similar form is provided in Chapter 7 for use with that form). This form may be used to include additional information and/or instructions for the attorney-in-fact.

Agent's Certification of the Validity of Power of Attorney and Agent's Authority: Finally, also included at the end of this chapter, is a form that may be used to verify an agent's authority to act under a particular power of attorney. This form may be presented to a financial institution in order to have a better chance that an agent's actions under a specific power of attorney will be accepted by the institution.

Selecting your Attorney-in-Fact (or Agent)

The person that you decide to choose as your attorney-in-fact or agent to act on your behalf must be someone that you trust implicitly. Depending on the type of power of attorney that you may use, this person will have a tremendous amount of authority over either your financial affairs or your health care decisions, or both. For any power of attorney, you will need to select someone that you know very well. Most often, you will select your spouse, if you are married. A trusted sibling or adult child may be another safe choice. For financial and business affairs, you will need someone who has the ability to understand such affairs and make prudent decisions on your behalf and in your best interests. For health care decisions, you will need to select someone who can understand medical situations and who has the ability to act solely on your behalf, without letting their own personal desires impact their decisions.

With the forms in this book, you are granting the appointed agent very broad powers to handle your affairs. You may give your agent the maximum power under law to perform the following specific acts on your behalf: all acts relating to any and all of your financial and/or business affairs, including all banking and financial institution transactions, all real estate transactions, all insurance and annuity transactions, all claims and litigation, and all business transactions. Your attorney-in-fact (agent) is granted full power to act on your behalf in the same manner as if you were personally present. This is not a power that should be conferred lightly. Very serious thought should be given to both who you appoint as your attorney-in-fact (the person you authorize to act on your behalf) and to any specific directions that you may want to give to that person regarding financial decisions. You do not have to appoint anyone to handle your financial or health care affairs on your behalf, but it is often very useful to do so.

By accepting their appointment, your agent agrees to act in your best interest as he or she considers advisable. For financial powers of attorney, your appointed agent agrees to keep your assets separate from their own and to exercise reasonable prudence in handling your affairs. The appointed agent also agrees to keep full and accurate records of any actions or transactions taken on your behalf. They also agree to keep any receipts regarding any transactions. Any power of attorney, whether for financial matters or health care, may be revoked at any time and is automatically revoked on your death.

The forms in this book will allow you to select an alternate or successor agent, that is, someone to act on your behalf if the main agent that you have selected is not available. It is a good idea to do so, since there may be circumstances beyond your control that would prevent your first choice of agent from acting. Your successor or alternate agent must also be someone whom your trust totally to handle your affairs, either financial or health care.

Additionally, you may wish to appoint two or more agents to act at the same time. Generally, however, this is not a good idea, as the agents may not be able to agree on a course of action and such conflicts can render the power of attorney useless. If you do desire to appoint more than one agent, you may wish to simply prepare two or more separate powers of attorney and allow your chosen agents to act separately. However, unless your multiple agents know each other well and are willing to act together in unison, this also may not be such a good idea. It is preferable to appoint a single agent and then appoint successor or alternate agents who would only have authority to act if your main choice for agent is unable or unwilling to act.

At the beginning of each of the documents are notices regarding the use of the particular type of power of attorney. They clearly explain the importance of caution in the use of this form and are applicable to all states. Please read each carefully to decide which of these forms are appropriate for your situation. Please note that the two durable power of attorney forms and the health care power of attorney form provide a release for your attorney-in-fact to receive your medical records under the federal HIPAA regulations relating to the privacy of health care records. This does not confer any authority for your attorney-in-fact to make health care decisions on your behalf. The HIPAA release is for the purpose of allowing your attorney-in-fact to have access to your medical files for the purpose of paying or examining medical bills and charges.

Please also note that the state-specific advance health care forms in Chapter 10 *do not* contain a durable power of attorney for financial affairs. If you wish to have this type of document as part of your advance health care plans, you will need to complete either one of the durable power of attorney forms in Chapter 6 or a state-specific durable power of attorney form in Chapter 9.

Methods for Completing Your Powers of Attorney

Please note that there are two distinct methods provided in this book for completing a power of attorney using this book. Either method is legal and either method may be selected. There are different reasons for choosing each method and these are outlined below:

Prepare Individual Forms

You may choose to complete one or more of the generic forms that are contained in Chapters 3 through 7. This method may be chosen if:

- You desire to custom-tailor one or more of the forms to more closely fit your individual wishes and desires concerning the use of your power of attorney, or

- The details of the state-specific forms (explained below) do not fit your individual desires concerning the use of your power of attorney.

In a few states, the legislatures have not developed specific language for one or more of the forms. These instances are noted under the state's heading in the appendix of this book. In such situations, you should use the individual forms (in Chapters 3-7) for those states. Any such forms have been prepared following guidelines and requirements set out by the particular state's legislature.

These forms are provided on the enclosed CD in two separate formats: either as PDF forms that may be filled in on your computer, but not altered, or as text forms that may be carefully altered to more closely fit your individual wishes and desires. The individual forms have been prepared to meet the minimum legal requirements in all states and are legally-valid in all states. Please see the detailed instructions in Chapter 1 concerning how to complete either the PDF or text versions of these individual forms.

Prepare State-Specific Forms

The second method is to prepare a state-specific form in either Chapter 9 or 10. A '*state-specific form*' is a form that has been taken directly from the laws of your particular state or is based on the legislative requirements of a particular state. The legal effects of the language in such a document have been approved by the legislature of the state. This provides an advantage in that the legal language in such a 'statutory' form is generally familiar to most financial institutions (or health care providers, in the case of advance health care directives) in the particular state and they know that such language has been approved. This does not mean, however, that other 'non-statutory' forms are not legally valid in the state as well.

All states specifically provide, in their legislation regarding powers of attorney, that power of attorney forms other than those contained in the statute itself are legally-valid. Anyone may use a 'non-statutory' legal form, such as those in Chapters 3 through 7, with language that they find appropriate to their own situation, as long as the document meets certain minimum legal standards for a particular state. All of the forms in this book meet such required legal standards.

The state-specific advance health care directives that are explained in Chapter 10 of this book and are found on the CD (in fillable PDF format) have also been prepared directly from the language and/or legislative guidance found in the statutes of each individual state. They are designed as a complete advance health care directive containing all appropriate forms. Any such forms have been prepared following any guidelines set out by the state's legislature.

Witness and Notary Requirements

All states have provided protections to ensure the validity of the powers of attorney. They have also provided legal protections against persons using undue influence to force or coerce someone into signing a power of attorney—by requiring the use of witnesses to signatures and/or the use of a notary public to acknowledge the signature.

All of the forms included in this book, including all of the state-specific forms, are designed to be notarized. This is a requirement in most states for most forms and has been made mandatory on all of the forms in this book. The purpose of notarization in this instance is to add another level of protection against coercion or undue pressure being exerted to force anyone to sign any of these legal forms against their wishes. Sadly, such undue pressure has been applied in some cases to force senior citizens to sign legal documents against their own wishes. The requirement that one sign a document in front of a notary and in front of two additional witnesses can significantly lessen the opportunity for such abuse.

Preparing and Signing Your Power of Attorney

① Select the appropriate form from the included forms in Chapters 3-7 or select a state-specific form for your state from Chapters 9-10. Carefully read through the entire form selected. You may wish to make two copies of the form(s) that you choose. This will allow you to use one form as a draft copy and the other form for a final copy that you, your witnesses, and a notary will sign.

② For all forms, make the appropriate choices in each section where indicated by initialing the designated place or filling in the appropriate information. Depending on which form that you use, you may have many choices to initial or you may have no choices to initial. Please carefully read through the paragraphs and clauses that require choices to be certain that you understand the choices that you will be making. If you wish to add additional instructions or limitations in the places indicated on the form, please type or clearly print your instructions. Note: If you wish to add extensive additional instructions to any form, you will need to do so in two ways: a) the preferred method would be to use the text-formatted forms on the CD and insert such additional instructions directly into the form, or b) if you choose to use the PDF-formatted forms, you may add additional instructions by adding the phrase "See additional sheet which is attached to this document and incorporated by reference." A form for "Additional Information for Power of Attorney" is located at the end of this chapter. Please see the instructions for that form at the end of this chapter.

③ Finally, you will need to complete the signature and witness/notary sections of your forms. When you have a completed original with no erasures or corrections, staple all of the pages together in the upper left-hand corner. Do not sign this document or fill in the date yet. You should now assemble your witnesses and a notary public to witness your signature.

④ In front of all of the witnesses and the notary public, the following should take place in the order shown:

(a) There is no requirement that the witnesses (or notary) know any of the terms of your power of attorney or other legal forms, or that they read your power of attorney or legal forms. All that is necessary is that they observe you sign your power of attorney and that they also sign the power of attorney as witnesses in each other's presence. You will sign your legal form at the end where indicated, exactly as your name is written on the form, in ink using a pen. At this time, if you are using a form requiring initials in some spaces, you should also initial your choices as to which sections you have chosen. You will also need to fill in the date. Once you have signed and completed all of the necessary information, pass your legal form to the first witness, who should sign the acknowledgment where indicated and also print his or her name (in the witness section prior to the witness signature area).

(b) After the first witness has signed, have the legal form passed to the second witness, who should also sign the acknowledgment where indicated and print his or her name (in the witness section prior to the witness signature area).

(c) Throughout this ceremony, you and all of the witnesses must remain together. The final step is for the notary public to sign in the space where indicated and complete the notarization block on the form.

(d) If you have chosen individuals to act as either your health care agent (health care power of attorney) or as your attorney-in-fact for financial affairs (any other powers of attorney) and any successors agents, you should have them sign the form at the end where shown acknowledging that they accept their appointment. Note that these signature generally do not need to be witnessed or notarized.

⑤ When this step is completed, the individual legal form that you have signed is a valid legal document. Have several photo-copies made and, if appropriate, deliver a copy to any financial institutions that you intend to honor your power of attorney. (If you have completed a durable health care power of attorney or advance health care directive, provide your attending physician with a copy to have placed in your medical records file.) You should also provide a copy to any person who was selected as either your health care agent or your attorney-in-fact for financial affairs. You may also desire to give a copy to the person you have chosen as the executor of your will, your clergy, and your spouse or other trusted relative.

Important Note: Although most states have passed laws that require that persons or financial institutions honor the state-specific statutory forms that are provided in this book, not all institutions will do so. Unfortunately, Many financial institutions will require the use of their own power of attorney form.

Finally, after the following Power of Attorney Chart, you will find two additional forms that may be used with any of the power of attorney forms in this book: Additional Information for Power of Attorney form and Agent's Certification of the Validity of Power of Attorney and Agent's Authority.

Power of Attorney Chart:

Use this chart to determine your specific power of attorney needs

Type of Power of Attorney	Effective for Financial Affairs	Effective for Health Care Decisions	Effective Immediately	Effective if Incapacitated
Unlimited Power of Attorney	YES, for *any and all* financial and business affairs	NO	YES	NO
General Power of Attorney	YES, but *may* be limited to specific situations	NO	YES	NO
Limited Power of Attorney	YES, but must be limited to specific situations	NO	YES	NO
Limited Power of Attorney for Real Estate	YES, but limited to real estate transactions	NO	YES	NO
Limited Power of Attorney for Child Care	NO, limited to child care situations	YES, but limited to consent to emergency medical care	YES	YES, if child is incapacitated
Durable Unlimited Power of Attorney (effective immediately)	YES, for *any and all* financial and business affairs	NO	YES	YES
Durable Unlimited Power of Attorney (effective upon disability)	YES, for *any and all* financial and business affairs	NO	NO, only effective upon incapacity of principal	YES, only becomes effective upon incapacity
Durable Health Care Power of Attorney	NO, only effective for health care decisions	YES, only effective for health care decisions	NO, only effective upon incapacity of principal	YES, only becomes effective upon incapacity

Instructions for Additional Information for Power of Attorney

If you need to add additional pages to your power of attorney document, please use the form titled "Additional Information for Power of Attorney" which is provided on the following page and on the CD. If you need to use additional pages, be certain that you initial and date each added page and that you clearly label each additional page regarding which paragraph or section of the form to which it pertains. You should also note in the form itself that you are using additional pages by printing or writing "See attached Additional Information page, which is incorporated by reference" in the section of the form where you wish to insert additional instructions or information. Note that this form should be attached to the original power of attorney document prior to the signing and notarization of the original document.

To complete this document, fill in the following information:

① Date of original power of attorney
② Name and address of person who originally granted power (principal)
③ Name and address of person granted power (attorney-in-fact)
④ Detailed statement of any additional information or instructions in power of attorney (Be certain that you note the paragraph or section of the original power of attorney where the additional information or instructions will apply).
⑤ Initials of principal and date of power of attorney

Additional Information for Power of Attorney

The following information is incorporated by reference and is to be considered as a part of the Power of Attorney, dated ① _____, under which the following principal ② _____, appointed the following attorney-in-fact to act on his or her behalf ③ _____.

Principal must initial and date below and insert additional information here:
④

⑤ Initials of Principal _____   Date _____

Instructions for Agent's Certification of the Validity of Power of Attorney and Agent's Authority

This form is useful to authenticate an agent's authority to act under a power of attorney. It may be required by a financial or other institution in order for the agent's actions to be accepted as acts on behalf of the principal. The purpose of this form is to have the agent (attorney-in-fact) certify that the power of attorney is still valid and in effect. This certification will provide the institution with the agent's promise that, as far as he or she knows, the power of attorney is still valid and the agent has full authority to act under the particular power of attorney. Note that a copy of the original power of attorney should be attached to this form.

To complete this form, please fill in the following information:

① State and county in which certification is notarized
② Name of person who was originally granted the power by the principal (attorney-in-fact)
③ Name of person who originally granted the power to the agent (principal)
④ Date of original power of attorney
⑤ Agent's signature, date of signing of certification, agent's printed name and address
⑥ Notary block to be completed by notary
⑦ Name of person who prepared the form

Agent's Certification of the Validity of Power of Attorney and Agent's Authority

①
State of _____

County of_____

②I, _____ (printed name of Agent),

③certify that _____(printed name of Principal)
signed a Power of Attorney (a copy of the Power of Attorney is attached to this certification) on
④_____ (date), naming the undersigned as an agent or successor agent.

I further certify that to my knowledge:

(1) the Principal is alive and has not revoked the Power of Attorney or my authority to act under the Power of Attorney and that the Power of Attorney remains in full force and effect;

(2) if the Power of Attorney was drafted to become effective upon the happening of an event or contingency that such event or contingency has occurred; and

(3) if I was named as a successor agent that the initial or predecessor agent is no longer able to serve.

⑤

_____   _____
Agent's signature   Date

_____
Agent's printed name

_____
Agent's address

Notary Acknowledgment

⑥
This document was acknowledged before me on _____ (date),
by_____(name of Agent).

_____   (Seal, if any)
Signature of Notary   My commission expires: _____

⑦
This document prepared by:

_____

CHAPTER 3
General Power of Attorney

A general power of attorney allows you to authorize your agent (your "attorney in fact") to handle a few or all of your financial and/or business transactions. With this form, you are giving another person the right to manage your financial and/or business matters on your behalf. They are given the power to act exactly as you could. This, of course, is a very powerful grant of authority to someone else to act on your behalf. The person appointed must be someone that you fully trust to handle your affairs. The authority granted by this power of attorney may be revoked by you at any time and is automatically revoked if you die or become incapacitated or incompetent. If there is anything about this form that you do not understand, you should ask a lawyer to explain it to you. This power of attorney contains an important notice prior to the form itself. Please read this notice carefully before you complete this form. In general, this notice provides that you understand the following:

> The importance of the form
> That you are not giving up your own rights to handle your affairs
> That you may be giving your attorney-in-fact power to handle all or many of your affairs (including the right to handle bank accounts, sell or mortgage real estate, etc. if selected)
> That any powers you grant to your attorney-in-fact will not exist if you become disabled
> That you are not granting anyone the power to make medical or health care decisions for you
> That you may revoke this power of attorney at any time
> That if you are divorced or your marriage is annulled, this power of attorney will be invalid
> That you should appoint only someone who is reliable, trustworthy, and competent

When You Should Use a General Power of Attorney

A general power of attorney allows you to select any or all of a range of powers that you wish for your agent (attorney-in-fact) to have. This type of power of attorney can be used to authorize someone else to sign certain documents if you can not be present when the signatures are necessary. They can be used to authorize someone to handle any or all of the following possible matters:

> Real estate transactions;
> Goods and services transactions;
> Stock, bond, share and commodity transactions;
> Banking transactions;
> Business operating transactions;
> Insurance transactions;
> Estate transactions;
> Legal claims and litigation;
> Personal relationships and affairs;

Benefits from military service;
Records, reports and statements;
Retirement benefit transactions;
Making gifts to a spouse, children, parents and other descendants;
Tax matters.

Additionally, you may also authorize your attorney-in-fact to delegate any or all of the above powers to someone that your appointed attorney-in-fact selects. This option should only be taken if you trust your appointed attorney-in-fact totally to make such a decision only with your best interests in mind.

A general power of attorney is most useful if you wish to grant your agent some, but not all of the possible powers available to an agent. If you wish to grant full and complete authority to your agent, you should use an *unlimited power of attorney* instead. An unlimited power of attorney provides that your agent will have total authority to act on your behalf for all financial and/or business matters (but not for health care decisions). If you wish to provide a very limited power to your agent, you may wish to use a *limited power of attorney* instead of a general power of attorney. A limited power of attorney allows you to limit the power granted to a specific action or a specific date range. A general power of attorney is not valid if you become disabled or incapacitated. You must use a *'durable' power of attorney* for that purpose. In addition, a general power of attorney also can *not* be used for health care decisions. You must use a *durable health care power of attorney* for that purpose.

To complete your general power of attorney, please follow the instructions below. If you choose to use the form on the enclosed CD, simply fill in the required information in either the text or PDF versions of this form.

Instructions for General Power of Attorney

① Name and address of person granting power (principal)
② Name and address of person granted power (attorney-in-fact)
③ Initial each of the specific powers that you wish your attorney-in-fact to have. If you wish your attorney-in-fact to have full authority to do anything that you yourself could do, simply initial line (q). (Note: if you wish to have your attorney-in-fact to have full authority, you may wish to use the *unlimited power of attorney* form instead).
④ Name and address of successor to person originally granted power (successor attorney-in-fact) (optional-if not used, write n/a in this space)
⑤ Date
⑥ Printed name of principal, date of signing of power of attorney, and signature of principal (signed in front of notary public)
⑦ Printed names and signatures of witnesses (signed in front of notary public)
⑧ Notary acknowledgement should be completed by the notary public
⑨ Printed name, date, and signature of attorney-in-fact (need not be witnessed or notarized)
⑩ Printed name, date, and signature of successor attorney-in-fact (optional-if not used, write N/A in this space)(need not be witnessed or notarized)

General Power of Attorney

Notice: This is an important document. Before signing this document, you should know these important facts. By signing this document, you are not giving up any powers or rights to control your finances and property yourself. In addition to your own powers and rights, you may be giving another person, your attorney-in-fact, broad powers to handle your finances and property. This general power of attorney may give the person whom you designate (your "attorney-in-fact") broad powers to handle your finances and property, which may include powers to encumber, sell or otherwise dispose of any real or personal property without advance notice to you or approval by you. THE POWERS GRANTED WILL NOT EXIST AFTER YOU BECOME DISABLED, OR INCAPACITATED. This document does not authorize anyone to make medical or other health care decisions for you. If you own complex or special assets such as a business, or if there is anything about this form that you do not understand, you should ask a lawyer to explain this form to you before you sign it. If you wish to change your general power of attorney, you must complete a new document and revoke this one. You may revoke this document at any time by destroying it, by directing another person to destroy it in your presence or by signing a written and dated statement expressing your intent to revoke this document. If you revoke this document, you should notify your attorney-in-fact and any other person to whom you have given a copy of the form. You also should notify all parties having custody of your assets. These parties have no responsibility to you unless you actually notify them of the revocation. If your attorney-in-fact is your spouse and your marriage is annulled, or you are divorced after signing this document, this document is invalid. Since some 3rd parties or some transactions may not permit use of this document, it is advisable to check in advance, if possible, for any special requirements that may be imposed. You should sign this form only if the attorney-in-fact you name is reliable, trustworthy and competent to manage your affairs. This form must be signed by the Principal (the person appointing the attorneyin-fact), witnessed by two persons other than the notary public, and acknowledged by a notary public.

①I, _____(printed name) ,
of (address)_____,
as principal, to grant a general power of attorney to, and do hereby appoint:
②_____ (printed name),
of (address)_____,
my attorney-in-fact to act in my name, place and stead in any way which I myself could do, if I were personally present, with respect to the following matters to the extent that I am permitted by law to act through an agent:
③
_____ (a) real estate transactions;
_____ (b) goods and services transactions;
_____ (c) bond, share and commodity transactions;
_____ (d) banking transactions;
_____ (e) business operating transactions;
_____ (f) insurance transactions;
_____ (g) estate transactions;
_____ (h) claims and litigation;

_____ (i) personal relationships and affairs;

_____ (j) benefits from military service;

_____ (k) records, reports and statements;

_____ (l) retirement benefit transactions;

_____ (m) making gifts to my spouse, children and more remote descendants, and parents;

_____ (n) tax matters;

_____ (o) all other matters;

_____ (p) full and unqualified authority to my attorney-in-fact to delegate any or all of the foregoing powers to any person or persons whom my attorney-in-fact shall select;

_____ (q) unlimited power and authority to act in all of the above situations (a) through (p)

If the attorney-in-fact named above is unable or unwilling to serve, I appoint

④ _____ (printed name),

of (address) _____ ,

to be my attorney-in-fact for all purposes hereunder.

To induce any third party to rely upon this power of attorney, I agree that any third party receiving a signed copy or facsimile of this power of attorney may rely upon such copy, and that revocation or termination of this power of attorney shall be ineffective as to such third party until actual notice or knowledge of such revocation or termination shall have been received by such third party. I, for myself and for my heirs, executors, legal representatives and assigns, agree to indemnify and hold harmless any such third party from any and all claims that may arise against such third party by reason of such third party having relied on the provisions of this power of attorney. This power of attorney shall not be effective in the event of my future disability or incapacity. This power of attorney may be revoked by me at any time and is automatically revoked upon my death. My attorney-in-fact shall no be compensated for his or her services nor shall my attorney-in-fact be liable to me, my estate, heirs, successors, or assigns for acting or refraining from acting under this document, except for willful misconduct or gross negligence.

⑤ Dated: _____

⑥ Signature and Declaration of Principal

I, _____ (printed name) , the principal, sign my name to this power of attorney this _____ day of _____ and, being first duly sworn, do declare to the undersigned authority that I sign and execute this instrument as my power of attorney and that I sign it willingly, or willingly direct another to sign for me, that I execute it as my free and voluntary act for the purposes expressed in the power of attorney and that I am eighteen years of age or older, of sound mind and under no constraint or undue influence.

_____

Signature of Principal

⑦ Witness Attestation

I, _____ (printed name), the first witness,

and I, _____ (printed name), the second witness, sign my name to the foregoing power of attorney being first duly sworn and do declare to the undersigned authority that the principal signs and executes this instrument as his/her power of attorney and that he\she signs it willingly, or willingly directs another to sign for him/her, and that I, in the presence and hearing of the principal, sign this power of attorney as witness to the principal's signing and that to the best of my knowledge the principal is eighteen years of age or older, of sound mind and under no constraint or undue influence.

_____

Signature of First Witness

_____

Signature of Second Witness

⑧ Notary Acknowledgment

State of _____ County of _____
Subscribed, sworn to and acknowledged before me by _____,
the Principal, and subscribed and sworn to before me by _____
and _____, the witnesses, this _____ day of
_____ .

_____

Notary Signature
Notary Public,
In and for the County of _____ State of _____
My commission expires: _____ Seal

⑨ Acknowledgment and Acceptance of Appointment as Attorney-in-Fact

I, _____, (printed name) have read the attached power of attorney and am the person identified as the attorney-in-fact for the principal. I hereby acknowledge that I accept my appointment as attorney-in-fact and that when I act as agent I shall exercise the powers for the benefit of the principal; I shall keep the assets of the principal separate from my assets; I shall exercise reasonable caution and prudence; and I shall keep a full and accurate record of all actions, receipts and disbursements on behalf of the principal.

_____   _____

Signature of Attorney-in-Fact   Date

⑩ Acknowledgment and Acceptance of Appointment as Successor Attorney-in-Fact

I, _____, (printed name) have read the attached power of attorney and am the person identified as the successor attorney-in-fact for the principal. I hereby acknowledge that I accept my appointment as successor attorney-in-fact and that, in the absence of a specific provision to the contrary in the power of attorney, when I act as agent I shall exercise the powers for the benefit of the principal; I shall keep the assets of the principal separate from my assets; I shall exercise reasonable caution and prudence; and I shall keep a full and accurate record of all actions, receipts and disbursements on behalf of the principal.

_____   _____

Signature of Successor Attorney-in-Fact   Date

CHAPTER 4
Unlimited Power of Attorney

An unlimited power of attorney should be used only in situations where you desire to authorize another person to act for you in *any and all* transactions. The grant of power under this document is unlimited. However, the powers you grant with this document cease to be effective should you become disabled or incompetent. This form gives the person whom you designate as your "attorney-in-fact" extremely broad powers to handle your property during your lifetime, which may include powers to mortgage, sell, or otherwise dispose of any real or personal property without advance notice to you or approval by you. This document does not authorize anyone to make medical or other health care decisions. You must execute a durable health care power of attorney to do this. The authority granted by this power of attorney may be revoked by you at any time and is automatically revoked if you die or become incapacitated or incompetent. If there is anything about this form that you do not understand, you should ask a lawyer to explain it to you. This power of attorney contains an important notice prior to the form itself. Please read this notice carefully before you complete this form. In general, this notice provides that you understand the following:

> The importance of the form
> That you are not giving up your own rights to handle your affairs
> That you are giving your attorney-in-fact power to handle all of your affairs without your consent (including the right to handle bank accounts, sell or mortgage real estate, etc.)
> That any powers you grant to your attorney-in-fact will not exist if you become disabled
> That you are not granting anyone the power to make medical or health care decisions for you
> That you may revoke this power of attorney at any time
> That if you are divorced or your marriage is annulled, this power of attorney will be invalid
> That you should appoint only someone who is reliable, trustworthy, and competent

When You Should Use an Unlimited Power of Attorney

An unlimited power of attorney authorizes your agent to handle *any and all* of your financial and business affairs, including all of the following possible matters:

> Real estate transactions;
> Personal property and goods and services transactions;
> Stock, bond, share and commodity transactions;
> Banking and financial institution transactions;
> Business operating transactions;
> Insurance and annuity transactions;
> Estate, trust, and other transactions where the principal is a beneficiary;
> Legal claims and litigation;

Personal and family maintenance;
Benefits from social security, medicare, medicaid, or civil or military service;
Records, reports and statements;
Retirement benefit transactions;
Tax matters;
Delegation of the agent's authority to others;
and any and all other matters.

All of the above mentioned powers that are granted to your agent are spelled out in great detail in this particular power of attorney form. This is the most extensive and detailed power of attorney form that is provided. It should only be used if you are absolutely certain that the agent you choose is fully and totally trustworthy and able to exercise these broad powers in your best interest. The detailed powers that are listed in this form are taken from the Uniform Power of Attorney Act that has been legislatively adopted by many states. Please note that the "delegation of the agent's authority to others" provision in this document grants your chosen agent the power to delegate any of his or her powers to another person of his or her own choosing. If you do not wish your agent to have this authority, or you wish to limit your agent's power under any of the other powers which are enumerated in this document, you should use instead a *general power of attorney*. A general power of attorney will allow you to pick and choose which of these powers you wish to grant to your agent. If you wish to provide a very limited power to your agent, you may wish to use a *limited power of attorney* instead of an unlimited power of attorney. A limited power of attorney allows you to limit the power granted to a specific action or a specific date range. An unlimited power of attorney is not valid if you become disabled or incapacitated. You must use a *'durable' power of attorney* for that purpose. In addition, an unlimited power of attorney also can *not* be used for health care decisions. You must use a *durable health care power of attorney* for that purpose.

To complete your unlimited power of attorney, please follow the instructions below. If you choose to use the form on the enclosed CD, simply fill in the required information in either the text or PDF versions of this form.

Instructions for Unlimited Power of Attorney

① Name and address of person granting power (principal)
② Name and address of person granted power (attorney-in-fact)
③ Name and address of successor to person originally granted power (successor attorney-in-fact) (optional-if not used, write N/A in this space)
④ Date
⑤ Printed name of principal, date of signing of power of attorney, and signature of principal (signed in front of notary public)
⑥ Printed names and signatures of witnesses (signed in front of notary public)
⑦ Notary acknowledgement should be completed by the notary public
⑧ Printed name, date, and signature of attorney-in-fact (need not be witnessed or notarized)
⑨ Printed name, date, and signature of successor attorney-in-fact (optional-if not used, write N/A in this space) (need not be witnessed or notarized)

Unlimited Power of Attorney

Notice: This is an important document. Before signing this document, you should know these important facts. By signing this document, you are not giving up any powers or rights to control your finances and property yourself. In addition to your own powers and rights, you are giving another person, your attorney-in-fact, broad powers to handle your finances and property. This unlimited power of attorney will give the person whom you designate (your "attorney-in-fact") broad powers to handle your finances and property, which includes powers to encumber, sell or otherwise dispose of any real or personal property without advance notice to you or approval by you. THE POWERS GRANTED WILL NOT EXIST AFTER YOU BECOME DISABLED, OR INCAPACITATED. This document does not authorize anyone to make medical or other health care decisions for you. If you own complex or special assets such as a business, or if there is anything about this form that you do not understand, you should ask a lawyer to explain this form to you before you sign it. If you wish to change your unlimited power of attorney, you must complete a new document and revoke this one. You may revoke this document at any time by destroying it, by directing another person to destroy it in your presence or by signing a written and dated statement expressing your intent to revoke this document. If you revoke this document, you should notify your attorney-in-fact and any other person to whom you have given a copy of the form. You also should notify all parties having custody of your assets. These parties have no responsibility to you unless you actually notify them of the revocation. If your attorney-in-fact is your spouse and your marriage is annulled, or you are divorced after signing this document, this document is invalid. Since some 3rd parties or some transactions may not permit use of this document, it is advisable to check in advance, if possible, for any special requirements that may be imposed. You should sign this form only if the attorney-in-fact you name is reliable, trustworthy and competent to manage your affairs. This form must be signed by the Principal (the person appointing the attorney-in-fact), witnessed by two persons other than the notary public, and acknowledged by a notary public.

①I, _____ (printed name),
of (address)_____,
as principal, do grant an unlimited power of attorney to, and do hereby appoint:
② _____(printed name),
of (address)_____,
my attorney-in-fact and do grant him or her unlimited power and authority to act in my name, place and stead in any way which I myself could do, if I were personally present, with respect to all of the following matters to the extent that I am permitted by law to act through an agent:

IN GENERAL, the principal authorizes the agent to: (1) demand, receive, and obtain by litigation or otherwise, money or other thing of value to which the principal is, may become, or claims to be entitled, and conserve, invest, disburse, or use anything so received for the purposes intended; (2) contract in any manner with any person, on terms agreeable to the agent, to accomplish a purpose of a transaction, and perform, rescind, reform, release, or modify the contract or another contract made by or on behalf of the principal; (3) execute, acknowledge, seal, and deliver a deed, revocation, mortgage, security agreement, lease, notice, check, promissory note, electronic funds transfer, release, or other instrument or communication the agent considers desirable to accomplish a purpose of a transaction, including creating a schedule of the principal's property and attaching it to the power of attorney; (4) prosecute, defend, submit to arbitration or mediation, settle, and propose or accept a compromise with respect to, a claim existing in favor of or against the principal or intervene in litigation relating to the claim; (5) seek on the principal's behalf the assistance of a court to carry out an act authorized by the principal in the power of attorney; (6) engage, compensate, and discharge an attorney, accountant, expert witness, or other assistant; (7) keep appropriate records of each transaction, including an accounting of receipts and disbursements; (8) prepare, execute, and file a record, report, or other document the agent considers desirable to safeguard or promote the principal's interest under a statute or governmental regulation; (9) reimburse the agent for expenditures properly made by the agent in exercising the powers granted by the power of attorney; and (10) in general, do any other lawful act with respect to the power and all property related to the power.

WITH RESPECT TO REAL PROPERTY, the principal authorizes the agent to: (1) accept as a gift or as security for an extension of credit, reject, demand, buy, lease, receive, or otherwise acquire, an interest in real property or a right incident to real property; (2) sell, exchange, convey with or without covenants, quitclaim, release, surrender, mortgage, retain title for security, encumber, partition, consent to partitioning, subdivide, apply for zoning, rezoning, or other governmental permits, plat or consent to platting, develop, grant options concerning, lease, sublease, or otherwise dispose of, an interest in real property or a right incident to real property; (3) release, assign, satisfy, or enforce by litigation or otherwise, a mortgage, deed of trust, conditional sale contract, encumbrance, lien, or other claim to real property which exists or is asserted; (4) manage or conserve an interest in real property or a right incident to real property, owned or claimed to be owned by the principal, including: (a) insuring against a casualty, liability, or loss; (b) obtaining or regaining possession, or protecting the interest or right, by litigation or otherwise; (c) paying, compromising, or contesting taxes or assessments, or applying for and receiving refunds in connection with them; and (d) purchasing supplies, hiring assistance or labor, and making repairs or alterations to the real property; (5) use, develop, alter, replace, remove, erect, or install structures or other improvements upon real property in or incident to which the principal has, or claims to have, an interest or right; (6) participate in a reorganization with respect to real property or a legal entity that owns an interest in or right incident to real property and receive and hold, directly or indirectly, shares of stock or obligations, or other evidences of ownership or debt, received in a plan of reorganization, and act with respect to them, including: (a) selling or otherwise disposing of them; (b) exercising or selling an option, conversion, or similar right with respect to them; and (c) voting them in person or by proxy; (7) change the form of title of an interest in or right incident to real property, and (8) dedicate to public use, with or without consideration, easements or other real property in which the principal has, or claims to have, an interest.

WITH RESPECT TO TANGIBLE PERSONAL PROPERTY, the principal authorizes the agent to: (1) accept as a gift or as security for an extension of credit, reject, demand, buy, receive, or otherwise acquire ownership or possession of tangible personal property or an interest in tangible personal property; (2) sell, exchange, convey with or without covenants, release, surrender, create a security interest in, grant options concerning, lease, sublease to others, or otherwise dispose of tangible personal property or an interest in tangible personal property; (3) release, assign, satisfy, or enforce by litigation or otherwise, a security interest, lien, or other claim on behalf of the principal, with respect to tangible personal property or an interest in tangible personal property; (4) manage or conserve tangible personal property or an interest in tangible personal property on behalf of the principal, including: (a) insuring against casualty, liability, or loss; (b) obtaining or regaining possession, or protecting the property or interest, by litigation or otherwise; (c) paying, compromising, or contesting taxes or assessments or applying for and receiving refunds in connection with taxes or assessments; (d) moving from place to place; (e) storing for hire or on a gratuitous bailment; and (f) using, altering, and making repairs or alterations; and (5) change the form of title of an interest in tangible personal property.

WITH RESPECT TO TRANSACTIONS CONCERNING STOCKS AND BONDS, the principal authorizes the agent to: (1) buy, sell, and exchange stocks, bonds, mutual funds, and all other types of securities and financial instruments, whether held directly or indirectly, except commodity futures contracts and call and put options on stocks and stock indexes, (2) receive certificates and other evidences of ownership with respect to securities, (3) exercise voting rights with respect to securities in person or by proxy, enter into voting trusts, and consent to limitations on the right to vote.

WITH RESPECT TO TRANSACTIONS CONCERNING COMMODITIES AND OPTIONS, the principal authorizes the agent to: (1) buy, sell, exchange, assign, settle, and exercise commodity futures contracts and call and put options on stocks and stock indexes traded on a regulated option exchange, and (2) establish, continue, modify, and terminate option accounts with a broker.

WITH RESPECT TO TRANSACTIONS CONCERNING BANKS AND OTHER FINANCIAL INSTITUTIONS, the principal authorizes the agent to: (1) continue, modify, and terminate an account or other banking arrangement made by or on behalf of the principal; (2) establish, modify, and terminate an account or other banking arrangement with a bank, trust company, savings and loan association, credit union, thrift company, brokerage firm, or other financial institution selected by the agent; (3) rent a safe deposit box or space in a vault; (4) contract for other services available from a financial institution as the agent considers desirable; (5) withdraw by check, order, or otherwise money or property of the principal deposited with or left in the custody of a financial institution; 6) receive bank statements, vouchers, notices, and similar documents from a financial institution and act with respect to them; (7) enter a safe deposit box or vault and withdraw or add to the contents; (8) borrow money at an interest rate agreeable to the agent and pledge as security personal property of the principal necessary in order to borrow, pay, renew, or extend the time of payment of a debt of the principal; (9) make, assign, draw, endorse, discount, guarantee, and negotiate promissory notes, checks, drafts, and other negotiable or nonnegotiable paper of the principal, or payable to the principal or the principal's order, transfer money, receive the cash or other proceeds of those transactions, accept a draft drawn by a person upon the principal, and pay it when due; (10) receive for the principal and act upon a sight draft, warehouse receipt, or other negotiable or nonnegotiable instrument; (11) apply for, receive, and use letters of credit, credit and debit cards, and traveler's checks from a financial institution and give an indemnity or other agreement in connection with letters of credit; and (12) consent to an extension of the time of payment with respect to commercial paper or a financial transaction with a financial institution.

WITH RESPECT TO OPERATING A BUSINESS, the principal authorizes the agent to: (1) operate, buy, sell, enlarge, reduce, and terminate a business interest; (2) act for a principal, subject to the terms of a partnership agreement or operating agreement, to: (a) perform a duty or discharge a liability and exercise a right, power, privilege, or option that the principal has, may have, or claims to have, under the partnership agreement or operating agreement, whether or not the principal is a partner in a partnership or member of a limited liability company; (b) enforce the terms of the partnership agreement or operating agreement by litigation or otherwise; and (c) defend, submit to arbitration, settle, or compromise litigation to which the principal is a party because of membership in a partnership or limited liability company; (3) exercise in person or by proxy, or enforce by litigation or otherwise, a right, power, privilege, or option the principal has or claims to have as the holder of a bond, share, or other instrument of similar character and defend, submit to arbitration or mediation, settle, or compromise litigation to which the principal is a party because of a bond, share, or similar instrument; (4) with respect to a business controlled by the principal: (a) continue, modify, renegotiate, extend, and terminate a contract made by or on behalf of the principal with respect to the business before execution of the power of attorney; (b) determine: (i) the location of its operation; (ii) the nature and extent of its business; (iii) the methods of manufacturing, selling, merchandising, financing, accounting, and advertising employed in its operation; (iv) the amount and types of insurance carried; and (v) the mode of engaging, compensating, and dealing with its accountants, attorneys, other agents, and employees; (c) change the name or form of organization under which the business is operated and enter into a partnership agreement or operating agreement with other persons or organize a corporation or other business entity to take over all or part of the operation of the business; and (d) demand and receive money due or claimed by the principal or on the principal's behalf in the operation of the business, and control and disburse the money in the operation of the business; (5) put additional capital into a business in which the principal has an interest; (6) join in a plan of reorganization, consolidation, or merger of the business; (7) sell or liquidate a business or part of it at the time and upon the terms the agent considers desirable; (8) establish the value of a business under a buy-out agreement to which the principal is a party; (9) prepare, sign, file, and deliver reports, compilations of information, returns, or other papers with respect to a business which are required by a governmental agency or instrumentality or which the agent considers desirable, and make related payments; and (10) pay, compromise, or contest taxes or assessments and perform any other act that the agent considers desirable to protect the principal from illegal or unnecessary taxation, fines, penalties, or assessments with respect to a business, including attempts to recover, in any manner permitted by law, money paid before or after the execution of the power of attorney.

WITH RESPECT TO INSURANCE AND ANNUITIES, the principal authorizes the agent to: (1) continue, pay the premium or assessment on, modify, rescind, release, or terminate a contract procured by or on behalf of the principal which insures or provides an annuity to either the principal or another person, whether or not the principal is a beneficiary under the contract; (2) procure new, different, and additional contracts of insurance and annuities for the principal and the principal's spouse, children, and other dependents, and select the amount, type of insurance or annuity, and mode of payment; (3) pay the premium or assessment on, modify, rescind, release, or terminate a contract of insurance or annuity procured by the agent; (4) apply for and receive a loan on the security of a contract of insurance or annuity; (5) surrender and receive the cash surrender value; (6)

exercise an election; (7) change the manner of paying premiums; (8) change or convert the type of insurance or annuity, with respect to which the principal has or claims to have a power described in this section; (9) apply for and procure government aid to guarantee or pay premiums of a contract of insurance on the life of the principal; (10) collect, sell, assign, hypothecate, borrow upon, or pledge the interest of the principal in a contract of insurance or annuity; and (11) pay from proceeds or otherwise, compromise or contest, and apply for refunds in connection with, a tax or assessment levied by a taxing authority with respect to a contract of insurance or annuity or its proceeds or liability accruing by reason of the tax or assessment.

WITH RESPECT TO ESTATES, TRUSTS, AND OTHER RELATIONSHIPS IN WHICH THE PRINCIPAL IS A BENEFICIARY, the principal authorizes the agent to act for the principal in all matters that affect a trust, probate estate, guardianship, conservatorship, escrow, custodianship, or other fund from which the principal is, may become, or claims to be entitled, as a beneficiary, to a share or payment, including to: (1) accept, reject, disclaim, receive, receipt for, sell, assign, release, pledge, exchange, or consent to a reduction in or modification of a share in or payment from the fund; (2) demand or obtain by litigation or otherwise money or other thing of value to which the principal is, may become, or claims to be entitled by reason of the fund; (3) initiate, participate in, and oppose litigation to ascertain the meaning, validity, or effect of a deed, will, declaration of trust, or other instrument or transaction affecting the interest of the principal; (4) initiate, participate in, and oppose litigation to remove, substitute, or surcharge a fiduciary; (5) conserve, invest, disburse, and use anything received for an authorized purpose; and (6) transfer an interest of the principal in real property, stocks, bonds, accounts with financial institutions or securities intermediaries, insurance, annuities, and other property, to the trustee of a revocable trust created by the principal as settlor.

WITH RESPECT TO CLAIMS AND LITIGATION, the principal authorizes the agent to: (1) assert and prosecute before a court or administrative agency a claim, a claim for relief, cause of action, counterclaim, offset, or defense against an individual, organization, or government, including actions to recover property or other thing of value, to recover damages sustained by the principal, to eliminate or modify tax liability, or to seek an injunction, specific performance, or other relief; (2) bring an action to determine adverse claims, intervene in litigation, and act as amicus curiae; (3) in connection with litigation, procure an attachment, garnishment, libel, order of arrest, or other preliminary, provisional, or intermediate relief and use an available procedure to effect or satisfy a judgment, order, or decree; (4) in connection with litigation, perform any lawful act, including acceptance of tender, offer of judgment, admission of facts, submission of a controversy on an agreed statement of facts, consent to examination before trial, and binding the principal in litigation; (5) submit to arbitration or mediation, settle, and propose or accept a compromise with respect to a claim or litigation; (6) waive the issuance and service of process upon the principal, accept service of process, appear for the principal, designate persons upon whom process directed to the principal may be served, execute and file or deliver stipulations on the principal's behalf, verify pleadings, seek appellate review, procure and give surety and indemnity bonds, contract and pay for the preparation and printing of records and briefs, receive and execute and file or deliver a consent, waiver, release, confession of judgment, satisfaction of judgment, notice, agreement, or other instrument in connection with the prosecution, settlement, or defense of a claim or litigation; (7) act for the principal with respect to bankruptcy or insolvency, whether voluntary or involuntary, concerning the principal or some other person, or with respect to a reorganization, receivership, or application for the appointment of a receiver or trustee which affects an interest of the principal in property or other thing of value; and (8) pay a judgment against the principal or a settlement made in connection with litigation and receive and conserve money or other thing of value paid in settlement of or as proceeds of a claim or litigation.

WITH RESPECT TO PERSONAL AND FAMILY MAINTENANCE, the principal authorizes the agent to: (1) perform the acts necessary to maintain the customary standard of living of the principal, the principal's spouse, children, and other individuals customarily or legally entitled to be supported by the principal, including providing living quarters by purchase, lease, or other contract, or paying the operating costs, including interest, amortization payments, repairs, and taxes, on premises owned by the principal and occupied by those individuals; (2) provide for the individuals described under (1) normal domestic help, usual vacations and travel expenses, and funds for shelter, clothing, food, appropriate education, and other current living costs; (3) pay on behalf of the individuals described under (1) expenses for necessary medical, dental, and surgical care, hospitalization, and custodial care; (4) act as the principal's personal representative pursuant to sections 1171 through 1179 of the Social Security Act, 42 U.S.C. Section 1320d (sections 262 and 264 of Public Law 104-191) [or successor provisions] and applicable regulations, in making decisions related to the past, present, or future payment for the provision of health care consented to by the principal or anyone authorized under the law of this state to consent to health care on behalf of the principal; (5) continue any provision made by the principal, for the individuals described under (1), for automobiles or other means of transportation, including registering, licensing, insuring, and replacing them; (6) maintain or open charge accounts for the convenience of the individuals described under (1) and open new accounts the agent considers desirable to accomplish a lawful purpose; and (7) continue payments incidental to the membership or affiliation of the principal in a church, club, society, order, or other organization or to continue contributions to those organizations.

WITH RESPECT TO BENEFITS FROM SOCIAL SECURITY, MEDICARE, MEDICAID, OTHER GOVERNMENTAL PROGRAMS, OR CIVIL OR MILITARY SERVICE, the principal authorizes the agent to: (1) execute vouchers in the name of the principal for allowances and reimbursements payable by the United States or a foreign government or by a state or subdivision of a state to the principal, including allowances and reimbursements for transportation of the individuals described in Section 212(1), and for shipment of their household effects; (2) take possession and order the removal and shipment of property of the principal from a post, warehouse, depot, dock, or other place of storage or safekeeping, either governmental or private, and execute and deliver a release, voucher, receipt, bill of lading, shipping ticket, certificate, or other instrument for that purpose; (3) prepare, file, and prosecute a claim of the principal to a benefit or assistance, financial or otherwise, to which the principal claims to be entitled under a statute or governmental regulation; (4) prosecute, defend, submit to arbitration or mediation, settle, and propose or accept a compromise with respect to any benefit or assistance the principal may be entitled to receive under a statute or governmental regulation; and (5) receive the financial proceeds of a claim of the type described in paragraph (3) and conserve, invest, disburse, or use anything so received for a lawful purpose.

WITH RESPECT TO RETIREMENT PLANS, the principal authorizes the agent to: (1) select a payment option under a retirement plan in which the principal participates, including a plan for a self-employed individual; (2) make voluntary contributions to those plans; (3) exercise the investment powers available under a self-directed retirement plan; (4) make a rollover of benefits into another retirement plan; (5) if authorized by the plan, borrow from, sell assets to, purchase assets from, or request distributions from the plan; and (6) waive the right of the principal to be a beneficiary of a joint or survivor annuity if the principal is a spouse who is not employed.

WITH RESPECT TO TAX MATTERS, the principal authorizes the agent to: (1) prepare, sign, and file federal, state, local, and foreign income, gift, payroll, Federal Insurance Contributions Act, and other tax returns, claims for refunds, requests for extension of time, petitions regarding tax matters, and any other tax-related documents, including receipts, offers, waivers, consents, including consents and agreements under the Internal Revenue Code, 26 U.S.C. Section 2032A [or successor provisions], closing agreements, and any power of attorney required by the Internal Revenue Service or other taxing authority with respect to a tax year upon which the statute of limitations has not run and the following 25 tax years; (2) pay taxes due, collect refunds, post bonds, receive confidential information, and contest deficiencies determined by the Internal Revenue Service or other taxing authority; (3) exercise any election available to the principal under federal, state, local, or foreign tax law; and (4) act for the principal in all tax matters for all periods before the Internal Revenue Service, and any other taxing authority.

WITH RESPECT TO GIFTS, the principal authorizes the agent to make gifts of any of the principal's property to individuals or organizations within the limits of the annual exclusion under the Internal Revenue Code, 26 U.S.C. Section 2503(b) [or successor provisions], as the agent determines to be in the principal's best interest based on all relevant factors, including: (1) the value and nature of the principal's property; (2) the principal's foreseeable obligations and need for maintenance; 3) minimization of income, estate, inheritance, generation-skipping transfer or gift taxes; (4) eligibility for public benefits or assistance under a statute or governmental regulation; and (5) the principal's personal history of making or joining in making gifts.

WITH RESPECT TO DELEGATION OF AGENCY AUTHORITY, the principal authorizes the agent to delegate revocably by writing or other record to one or more persons a power granted to the agent by the principal.

If the attorney-in-fact named above is unable or unwilling to serve, I appoint
③_____ (printed name),
of (address) _____ ,
to be my attorney-in-fact for all purposes hereunder.

To induce any third party to rely upon this power of attorney, I agree that any third party receiving a signed copy or facsimile of this power of attorney may rely upon such copy, and that revocation or termination of this power of attorney shall be ineffective as to such third party until actual notice or knowledge of such revocation or termination shall have been received by such third party. I, for myself and for my heirs, executors, legal representatives and assigns, agree to indemnify and hold harmless any such third party from any and all claims that may arise against such third party by reason of such third party having relied on the provisions of this power of attorney. This power of attorney shall not be effective in the event of my future disability or incapacity. This power of attorney may be revoked by me at any time and is automatically revoked upon my death. My attorney-in-fact shall no be compensated for his or her services nor shall my attorney-in-fact be liable to me, my estate, heirs, successors, or assigns for acting or refraining from acting under this document, except for willful misconduct or gross negligence.

④ Dated: _____

Signature and Declaration of Principal

⑤

I, _____ (printed name), the principal, sign my name to this power of attorney this _____ day of _____ and, being first duly sworn, do declare to the undersigned authority that I sign and execute this instrument as my power of attorney and that I sign it willingly, or willingly direct another to sign for me, that I execute it as my free and voluntary act for the purposes expressed in the power of attorney and that I am eighteen years of age or older, of sound mind and under no constraint or undue influence.

_____
Signature of Principal

Witness Attestation

⑥

I, _____ (printed name), the first witness, and I, _____ (printed name), the second witness, sign my name to the foregoing power of attorney being first duly sworn and do declare to the undersigned authority that the principal signs and executes this instrument as his/her power of attorney and that he\she signs it willingly, or willingly directs another to sign for him/her, and that I, in the presence and hearing of the principal, sign this power of attorney as witness to the principal's signing and that to the best of my knowledge the principal is eighteen years of age or older, of sound mind and under no constraint or undue influence.

_____
Signature of First Witness

_____
Signature of Second Witness

Notary Acknowledgment

⑦

State of _____ County of _____
Subscribed, sworn to and acknowledged before me by _____,
the Principal, and subscribed and sworn to before me by _____,
and _____, the witnesses, this _____ day of
_____ .

_____
Notary Signature
Notary Public,
In and for the County of _____ State of _____
My commission expires: _____ Seal

Acknowledgment and Acceptance of Appointment as Attorney-in-Fact

⑧

I, _____, (printed name) have read the attached power of attorney and am the person identified as the attorney-in-fact for the principal. I hereby acknowledge that I accept my appointment as attorney-in-fact and that when I act as agent I shall exercise the powers for the benefit of the principal; I shall keep the assets of the principal separate from my assets; I shall exercise reasonable caution and prudence; and I shall keep a full and accurate record of all actions, receipts and disbursements on behalf of the principal.

_____   _____
Signature of Attorney-in-Fact   Date

Acknowledgment and Acceptance of Appointment as Successor Attorney-in-Fact

⑨

I, _____, (printed name) have read the attached power of attorney and am the person identified as the successor attorney-in-fact for the principal. I hereby acknowledge that I accept my appointment as successor attorney-in-fact and that, in the absence of a specific provision to the contrary in the power of attorney, when I act as agent I shall exercise the powers for the benefit of the principal; I shall keep the assets of the principal separate from my assets; I shall exercise reasonable caution and prudence; and I shall keep a full and accurate record of all actions, receipts and disbursements on behalf of the principal.

_____   _____
Signature of Successor Attorney-in-Fact   Date

CHAPTER 5
Limited Powers of Attorney

This document provides for a *limited* grant of authority to another person. It should be used in those situations when you need to authorize another person to act for you in a specific transaction or transactions. The type of acts that you authorize the other person to perform should be spelled out in detail to avoid confusion (for example, to sign any necessary forms to open a bank account). If desired, the dates when the power of attorney will be valid may also be specified. Two additional specialized limited powers of attorney are also provided in this chapter: 1) one specifically to be used for granting someone authority to act on your behalf in a real estate transaction, and 2) one for authorizing another person to make certain limited child care decisions on your behalf for one of your children. The authority granted by any of these limited powers of attorney may be revoked by you at any time and is automatically revoked if you die or become incapacitated or incompetent. This document does not authorize the appointed attorney-in-fact to make any decisions relating to medical or health care (Note, however, that the limited power of attorney for child care does authorize your appointed agent to consent to emergency medical treatment for a child). If there is anything about these forms that you do not understand, you should ask a lawyer to explain it to you. These powers of attorney contain an important notice prior to the form itself. Please read this notice carefully before you complete this form. In general, this notice provides that you understand the following:

> The importance of the form
> That you are not giving up your own rights to handle your affairs
> That you are giving your attorney-in-fact power to handle some of your affairs (including possibly the right to handle bank accounts, sell or mortgage real estate, etc.)
> That any powers you grant to your attorney-in-fact will not exist if you become disabled
> That you are not granting anyone the power to make medical or health care decisions for you
> That you may revoke this power of attorney at any time
> That if you are divorced or your marriage is annulled, this power of attorney will be invalid
> That you should appoint only someone who is reliable, trustworthy, and competent

When You Should Use a Limited Power of Attorney

A limited power of attorney allows you to select a specific power that you wish for your agent (attorney-in-fact) to have. This type of power of attorney can be used to authorize someone else to sign certain documents if you can not be present when the signatures are necessary. They can be used to authorize someone to handle any of the following possible matters:

> Real estate transactions; goods and services transactions; stock, bond, share and commodity transactions; banking transactions; business operating transactions; insurance

transactions; estate transactions; legal claims and litigation; personal relationships and affairs; benefits from military service; records, reports and statements; retirement benefit transactions; making gifts to a spouse, children, parents and other descendants; tax matters; and certain child care decisions, such as consent to emergency medical care.

A limited power of attorney is most useful if you wish to grant your agent only some, but not all of the possible powers available to an agent. If you wish to grant full and complete authority to your agent, you may wish to use an *unlimited power of attorney* instead. An unlimited power of attorney provides that your agent will have total authority to act on your behalf for all financial and/or business matters (but not for health care decisions). If you wish to provide a range of powers to your agent, you may wish to use a *general power of attorney* instead of a limited power of attorney. A limited power of attorney allows you to limit the power granted to a specific action or a specific date range. A limited power of attorney is not valid if you become disabled or incapacitated. You must use a *'durable' power of attorney* for that purpose (Note: you can prepare a *'durable' limited power of attorney*). In addition, a limited power of attorney also can *not* be used for health care decisions. You must use a *durable health care power of attorney* for that purpose.

In addition to the basic limited power of attorney that follows, two additional specialized limited powers of attorney are provided. The first is designed to be used to authorize someone to act on your behalf only for a limited real estate transaction (normally, a real estate closing). The other additional form provided is a limited power of attorney for child care. This form is designed to allow you to authorize someone to consent to emergency medical care for your child and/or to enroll your child in a school or child care facility and/or exercise additional child care rights. Please follow the instructions provided for the use of these forms prior to each form later in this chapter.

To complete a limited power of attorney, please follow the instructions below. If you choose to use the form on the enclosed CD, simply fill in the required information in either the text or PDF versions of this form.

Instructions for Limited Power of Attorney

(1) Name and address of person granting power (principal)
(2) Name and address of person granted power (attorney-in-fact)
(3) List specific acts that you want your attorney-in-fact to perform (be as detailed as possible)
(4) Name and address of successor to person originally granted power (successor attorney-in-fact) (optional-if not used, write N/A in this space.)
(5) Date
(6) Printed name of principal, date of signing of power of attorney, and signature of principal (signed in front of notary public)
(7) Printed names and signatures of witnesses (signed in front of notary public)
(8) Notary acknowledgement should be completed by the notary public
(9) Printed name, date, and signature of attorney-in-fact (need not be witnessed or notarized)
(10) Printed name, date, and signature of successor attorney-in-fact (optional-if not used, write N/A in this space) (need not be witnessed or notarized)

Limited Power of Attorney

Notice: This is an important document. Before signing this document, you should know these important facts. By signing this document, you are not giving up any powers or rights to control your finances and property yourself. In addition to your own powers and rights, you may be giving another person, your attorney-in-fact, broad powers to handle your finances and property. This limited power of attorney may give the person whom you designate (your "attorney-in-fact") broad powers to handle your finances and property, which may include powers to encumber, sell or otherwise dispose of any real or personal property without advance notice to you or approval by you. THE POWERS GRANTED WILL NOT EXIST AFTER YOU BECOME DISABLED, OR INCAPACITATED. This document does not authorize anyone to make medical or other health care decisions for you. If you own complex or special assets such as a business, or if there is anything about this form that you do not understand, you should ask a lawyer to explain this form to you before you sign it. If you wish to change your limited power of attorney, you must complete a new document and revoke this one. You may revoke this document at any time by destroying it, by directing another person to destroy it in your presence or by signing a written and dated statement expressing your intent to revoke this document. If you revoke this document, you should notify your attorney-in-fact and any other person to whom you have given a copy of the form. You also should notify all parties having custody of your assets. These parties have no responsibility to you unless you actually notify them of the revocation. If your attorney-in-fact is your spouse and your marriage is annulled, or you are divorced after signing this document, this document is invalid. Since some 3rd parties or some transactions may not permit use of this document, it is advisable to check in advance, if possible, for any special requirements that may be imposed. You should sign this form only if the attorney-in-fact that you appoint is reliable, trustworthy and competent to manage your affairs. This form must be signed by the Principal (the person appointing the attorney-in-fact), witnessed by two persons other than the notary public, and acknowledged by a notary public.

① I, _____ (printed name),
of (address)_____,
as principal, do grant a limited and specific power of attorney to, and do hereby appoint
② _____ (printed name),
of (address)_____,
to act as my attorney-in-fact and to have the full power and authority to perform only the following acts on my behalf to the same extent that I could do so personally if I were personally present, with respect to the following matter to the extent that I am permitted by law to act through an agent: (list specific acts) ③

If the attorney-in-fact named above is unable or unwilling to serve, I appoint

④ _____ (printed name),

of (address) _____ ,

to be my attorney-in-fact for all purposes hereunder.

To induce any third party to rely upon this power of attorney, I agree that any third party receiving a signed copy or facsimile of this power of attorney may rely upon such copy, and that revocation or termination of this power of attorney shall be ineffective as to such third party until actual notice or knowledge of such revocation or termination shall have been received by such third party. I, for myself and for my heirs, executors, legal representatives and assigns, agree to indemnify and hold harmless any such third party from any and all claims that may arise against such third party by reason of such third party having relied on the provisions of this power of attorney.

This power of attorney shall not be effective in the event of my future disability or incapacity. This limited grant of authority does not authorize my attorney-in-fact to make any decisions regarding my medical or health care. This power of attorney may be revoked by me at any time and is automatically revoked upon my death. My attorney-in-fact shall not be compensated for his or her services nor shall my attorney-in-fact be liable to me, my estate, heirs, successors, or assigns for acting or refraining from acting under this document, except for willful misconduct or gross negligence. My attorney-in-fact accepts this appointment and agrees to act in my best interest as he or she considers advisable. This grant of authority shall include the power and authority to perform any incidental acts which may be reasonably required in order to perform the specific acts stated above.

⑤

Dated: _____

Signature and Declaration of Principal

⑥

I, _____ (printed name), the principal, sign my name to this power of attorney this _____ day of _____ and, being first duly sworn, do declare to the undersigned authority that I sign and execute this instrument as my power of attorney and that I sign it willingly, or willingly direct another to sign for me, that I execute it as my free and voluntary act for the purposes expressed in the power of attorney and that I am eighteen years of age or older, of sound mind and under no constraint or undue influence.

_____

Signature of Principal

Witness Attestation

⑦

I, _____ (printed name), the first witness,

and I, _____ (printed name), the second witness,

sign my name to the foregoing power of attorney being first duly sworn and do declare to the undersigned authority that the principal signs and executes this instrument as his/her power of attorney and that he\she signs it willingly, or willingly directs another to sign for him/her, and that I, in the presence and hearing of the principal, sign this power of attorney as witness to the principal's signing and that to the best of my knowledge the principal is eighteen years of age or older, of sound mind and under no constraint or undue influence.

_____

Signature of First Witness

_____

Signature of Second Witness

Notary Acknowledgment
⑧

State of _____ County of _____

Subscribed, sworn to and acknowledged before me by _____,

the Principal, and subscribed and sworn to before me by _____,

and _____, the witnesses, this _____ day of

_____ .

_____

Notary Signature
Notary Public,
In and for the County of _____ State of _____
My commission expires: _____ Seal

Acknowledgment and Acceptance of Appointment as Attorney-in-Fact
⑨

I, _____, (printed name) have read the attached power of attorney and am the person identified as the attorney-in-fact for the principal. I hereby acknowledge that I accept my appointment as attorney-in-fact and that when I act as agent I shall exercise the powers for the benefit of the principal; I shall keep the assets of the principal separate from my assets; I shall exercise reasonable caution and prudence; and I shall keep a full and accurate record of all actions, receipts and disbursements on behalf of the principal.

_____   _____

Signature of Attorney-in-Fact   Date

Acknowledgment and Acceptance of Appointment as Successor Attorney-in-Fact
⑩

I, _____, (printed name) have read the attached power of attorney and am the person identified as the successor attorney-in-fact for the principal. I hereby acknowledge that I accept my appointment as successor attorney-in-fact and that, in the absence of a specific provision to the contrary in the power of attorney, when I act as agent I shall exercise the powers for the benefit of the principal; I shall keep the assets of the principal separate from my assets; I shall exercise reasonable caution and prudence; and I shall keep a full and accurate record of all actions, receipts and disbursements on behalf of the principal.

_____   _____

Signature of Successor Attorney-in-Fact   Date

Instructions for Limited Power of Attorney for Real Estate

(1) Name and address of person granting power (principal)

(2) Name and address of person granted power (attorney-in-fact)

(3) List specific acts (relating to real estate only) that you want your attorney-in-fact to perform. (Be as detailed as possible. You should include an exact legal description of the real estate covered by the power of attorney. You should also include an exact date or dates for the power of attorney to be effective, if desired. An example might be:

"Authority to sign any and all documents, on behalf of the principal, relating to the real estate closing to be held on June 4, 2008, for the following described real estate: Parcel 123 of the Smith Subdivision, as described on Warranty Deed recorded on Page 234 of Book 56 in Jones County, Missouri").

(4) Name and address of successor to person originally granted power (successor attorney-in-fact) (optional-if not used, write N/A in this space.)

(5) Date

(6) Printed name of principal, date of signing of power of attorney, and signature of principal (signed in front of notary public)

(7) Printed names and signatures of witnesses (signed in front of notary public)

(8) Notary acknowledgement should be completed by the notary public

(9) Printed name, date, and signature of attorney-in-fact (need not be witnessed or notarized)

(10) Printed name, date, and signature of successor attorney-in-fact (optional-if not used, write N/A in this space) (need not be witnessed or notarized)

Limited Power of Attorney for Real Estate

Notice: This is an important document. Before signing this document, you should know these important facts. By signing this document, you are not giving up any powers or rights to control your finances and property yourself. In addition to your own powers and rights, you may be giving another person, your attorney-in-fact, broad powers to handle your finances and property. This limited power of attorney may give the person whom you designate (your "attorney-in-fact") broad powers to handle your finances and property, which may include powers to encumber, sell or otherwise dispose of any real or personal property without advance notice to you or approval by you. THE POWERS GRANTED WILL NOT EXIST AFTER YOU BECOME DISABLED, OR INCAPACITATED. This document does not authorize anyone to make medical or other health care decisions for you. If you own complex or special assets such as a business, or if there is anything about this form that you do not understand, you should ask a lawyer to explain this form to you before you sign it. If you wish to change your limited power of attorney, you must complete a new document and revoke this one. You may revoke this document at any time by destroying it, by directing another person to destroy it in your presence or by signing a written and dated statement expressing your intent to revoke this document. If you revoke this document, you should notify your attorney-in-fact and any other person to whom you have given a copy of the form. You also should notify all parties having custody of your assets. These parties have no responsibility to you unless you actually notify them of the revocation. If your attorney-in-fact is your spouse and your marriage is annulled, or you are divorced after signing this document, this document is invalid. Since some 3rd parties or some transactions may not permit use of this document, it is advisable to check in advance, if possible, for any special requirements that may be imposed. You should sign this form only if the attorney-in-fact that you appoint is reliable, trustworthy and competent to manage your affairs. This form must be signed by the Principal (the person appointing the attorney-in-fact), witnessed by two persons other than the notary public, and acknowledged by a notary public.

① I, _____ (printed name),
of (address)_____,
as principal, do grant a limited and specific power of attorney to, and do hereby appoint
② _____ , of
(address)_____,
to act as my attorney-in-fact and to have the full power and authority to perform only the following acts on my behalf to the same extent that I could do so personally if I were personally present, with respect to the following real estate matter to the extent that I am permitted by law to act through an agent: (list specific acts) ③

If the attorney-in-fact named above is unable or unwilling to serve, I appoint

④ _____ (printed name),

of (address) _____ ,

to be my attorney-in-fact for all purposes hereunder.

To induce any third party to rely upon this power of attorney, I agree that any third party receiving a signed copy or facsimile of this power of attorney may rely upon such copy, and that revocation or termination of this power of attorney shall be ineffective as to such third party until actual notice or knowledge of such revocation or termination shall have been received by such third party. I, for myself and for my heirs, executors, legal representatives and assigns, agree to indemnify and hold harmless any such third party from any and all claims that may arise against such third party by reason of such third party having relied on the provisions of this power of attorney.

This power of attorney shall not be effective in the event of my future disability or incapacity. This limited grant of authority does not authorize my attorney-in-fact to make any decisions regarding my medical or health care. This power of attorney may be revoked by me at any time and is automatically revoked upon my death. My attorney-in-fact shall not be compensated for his or her services nor shall my attorney-in-fact be liable to me, my estate, heirs, successors, or assigns for acting or refraining from acting under this document, except for willful misconduct or gross negligence. My attorney-in-fact accepts this appointment and agrees to act in my best interest as he or she considers advisable. This grant of authority shall include the power and authority to perform any incidental acts which may be reasonably required in order to perform the specific acts stated above.

⑤
Dated: _____

Signature and Declaration of Principal

⑥
I, _____ (printed name), the principal, sign my name to this power of attorney this _____ day of _____ and, being first duly sworn, do declare to the undersigned authority that I sign and execute this instrument as my power of attorney and that I sign it willingly, or willingly direct another to sign for me, that I execute it as my free and voluntary act for the purposes expressed in the power of attorney and that I am eighteen years of age or older, of sound mind and under no constraint or undue influence.

_____

Signature of Principal

Witness Attestation

⑦
I, _____ (printed name), the first witness, and I, _____ (printed name), the second witness, sign my name to the foregoing power of attorney being first duly sworn and do declare to the undersigned authority that the principal signs and executes this instrument as his/her power of attorney and that he\she signs it willingly, or willingly directs another to sign for him/her, and that I, in the presence and hearing of the principal, sign this power of attorney as witness to the

principal's signing and that to the best of my knowledge the principal is eighteen years of age or older, of sound mind and under no constraint or undue influence.

_____
Signature of First Witness

_____
Signature of Second Witness

Notary Acknowledgment
⑧
State of _____ County of _____

Subscribed, sworn to and acknowledged before me by _____,

the Principal, and subscribed and sworn to before me by _____,

and _____, the witnesses, this _____ day of

_____ .

_____
Notary Signature
Notary Public,
In and for the County of _____ State of _____
My commission expires: _____ Seal

Acknowledgment and Acceptance of Appointment as Attorney-in-Fact
⑨
I, _____, (printed name) have read the attached power of attorney and am the person identified as the attorney-in-fact for the principal. I hereby acknowledge that I accept my appointment as attorney-in-fact and that when I act as agent I shall exercise the powers for the benefit of the principal; I shall keep the assets of the principal separate from my assets; I shall exercise reasonable caution and prudence; and I shall keep a full and accurate record of all actions, receipts and disbursements on behalf of the principal.

_____   _____
Signature of Attorney-in-Fact   Date

Acknowledgment and Acceptance of Appointment as Successor Attorney-in-Fact
⑩
I, _____, (printed name) have read the attached power of attorney and am the person identified as the successor attorney-in-fact for the principal. I hereby acknowledge that I accept my appointment as successor attorney-in-fact and that, in the absence of a specific provision to the contrary in the power of attorney, when I act as agent I shall exercise the powers for the benefit of the principal; I shall keep the assets of the principal separate from my assets; I shall exercise reasonable caution and prudence; and I shall keep a full and accurate record of all actions, receipts and disbursements on behalf of the principal.

_____   _____
Signature of Successor Attorney-in-Fact   Date

Instructions for Limited Power of Attorney for Child Care

① Name and address of person granting power (principal)

② Name, age, and address of the child over whom you wish the attorney-in-fact to have authority

③ Name and address of person granted the power (attorney-in-fact or agent)

④ Initial the specific acts that you want your attorney-in-fact to perform. Note: only three child care actions are permitted using this type of power of attorney: 1) the authority to consent to emergency medical care for the child and/or 2) the authority to enroll the child in a school or child care facility and/or 3) the authority to exercise the same parental rights that you may exercise. You may initial any or all of these powers. If you wish your attorney-in-fact to have all of these powers, you should initial all three of the spaces. Please also note that if you have more than one child that you wish to grant someone else authority to make such decisions for, you must prepare a separate limited power of attorney for child care for each child.

⑤ Name and address of successor to person originally granted power (successor attorney-in-fact) (optional-if not used, write N/A in this space.)

⑥ Date

⑦ Printed name of principal, date of signing of power of attorney, and signature of principal (signed in front of notary public)

⑧ Printed names and signatures of witnesses (signed in front of notary public)

⑨ Notary acknowledgement should be completed by the notary public

⑩ Printed name, date, and signature of attorney-in-fact (need not be witnessed or notarized)

⑪ Printed name, date, and signature of successor attorney-in-fact (optional-if not used, write N/A in this space) (need not be witnessed or notarized)

Limited Power of Attorney for Child Care

Notice: This is an important document. Before signing this document, you should know these important facts. By signing this document, you are not giving up any powers or rights to provide child care consent or make child care decisions yourself. In addition to your own powers and rights, you may be giving another person, your attorney-in-fact, powers to provide consent to emergency medical care for a child and/or authority to enroll a child in a school or child care facility and/or authority to exercise additional parental rights. THE POWERS GRANTED WILL NOT EXIST AFTER YOU BECOME DISABLED, OR INCAPACITATED. If there is anything about this form that you do not understand, you should ask a lawyer to explain this form to you before you sign it. If you wish to change your limited power of attorney, you must complete a new document and revoke this one. You may revoke this document at any time by destroying it, by directing another person to destroy it in your presence or by signing a written and dated statement expressing your intent to revoke this document. If you revoke this document, you should notify your attorney-in-fact and any other person to whom you have given a copy of the form. These parties have no responsibility to you unless you actually notify them of the revocation. Since some 3rd parties or some transactions may not permit use of this document, it is advisable to check in advance, if possible, for any special requirements that may be imposed. You should sign this form only if the attorney-in-fact that you appoint is reliable, trustworthy and competent to manage make the child care decisions that you are authorizing them to make. This form must be signed by the Principal (the person appointing the attorney-in-fact), witnessed by two persons other than the notary public, and acknowledged by a notary public.

① I, _____ (printed name), of (address)_____, as principal, and as parent of the following child,
② ____._____ (printed name of child), _____ (age of child), of (address)_____ _____

do grant a limited and specific power of attorney to, and do hereby appoint
③_____ (printed name), of (address)_____, to act as my attorney-in-fact and to have the full power and authority to perform only the following acts **that bear my initials,** on my behalf to the same extent that I could do so personally if I were personally present, with respect to the following matter to the extent that I am permitted by law to act through an agent:
④

_____ to consent to any necessary medical treatment for the above child, including any emergency medical treatment, surgery, medication, hospitalization, or any other necessary medical treatment; that may be required;

_____ to enroll and/or withdraw the above child from any school or child care facility;

_____ to exercise the same parental rights that I may personally exercise regarding the care, custody and control of the above child;

If the attorney-in-fact named above is unable or unwilling to serve, I appoint

⑤_____ (printed name),

of (address) _____ ,

to be my attorney-in-fact for all purposes hereunder.

To induce any third party to rely upon this power of attorney, I agree that any third party receiving a signed copy or facsimile of this power of attorney may rely upon such copy, and that revocation or termination of this power of attorney shall be ineffective as to such third party until actual notice or knowledge of such revocation or termination shall have been received by such third party. I, for myself and for my heirs, executors, legal representatives and assigns, agree to indemnify and hold harmless any such third party from any and all claims that may arise against such third party by reason of such third party having relied on the provisions of this power of attorney. This power of attorney shall not be effective in the event of my future disability or incapacity. This power of attorney may be revoked by me at any time and is automatically revoked upon my death. My attorney-in-fact shall not be compensated for his or her services, nor shall my attorney-in-fact be liable to me, my estate, heirs, successors, or assigns for acting or refraining from acting under this document, except for willful misconduct or gross negligence. My attorney-in-fact accepts this appointment and agrees to act in my and my child's best interest as he or she considers advisable. This grant of authority shall include the power and authority to perform any incidental acts which may be reasonably required in order to perform the specific acts stated above.

⑥

Dated: _____

Signature and Declaration of Principal

⑦

I, _____ (printed name), the principal, sign my name to this power of attorney this _____ day of _____ and, being first duly sworn, do declare to the undersigned authority that I sign and execute this instrument as my power of attorney and that I sign it willingly, or willingly direct another to sign for me, that I execute it as my free and voluntary act for the purposes expressed in the power of attorney and that I am eighteen years of age or older, of sound mind and under no constraint or undue influence.

_____

Signature of Principal

Witness Attestation

⑧

I, _____ (printed name), the first witness, and I, _____ (printed name), the second witness, sign my name to the foregoing power of attorney being first duly sworn and do declare to the undersigned authority that the principal signs and executes this instrument as his/her power of attorney and that he\she signs it willingly, or willingly directs another to sign for him/her, and that I, in the presence and hearing of the principal, sign this power of attorney as witness to the principal's signing and that to the best of my knowledge the principal is eighteen years of age or older, of sound mind and under no constraint or undue influence.

_____

Signature of First Witness

_____

Signature of Second Witness

Notary Acknowledgment
⑨

State of _____ County of _____

Subscribed, sworn to and acknowledged before me by _____,

the Principal, and subscribed and sworn to before me by _____,

and _____, the witnesses, this _____ day of

_____ .

_____

Notary Signature
Notary Public,
In and for the County of _____ State of _____
My commission expires: _____ Seal

Acknowledgment and Acceptance of Appointment as Attorney-in-Fact
⑩

I, _____, (printed name) have read the attached power of attorney and am the person identified as the attorney-in-fact for the principal. I hereby acknowledge that I accept my appointment as attorney-in-fact and that when I act as agent I shall exercise the powers for the benefit of the principal; I shall keep the assets of the principal separate from my assets; I shall exercise reasonable caution and prudence; and I shall keep a full and accurate record of all actions, receipts and disbursements on behalf of the principal.

_____   _____

Signature of Attorney-in-Fact   Date

Acknowledgment and Acceptance of Appointment as Successor Attorney-in-Fact
⑪

I, _____, (printed name) have read the attached power of attorney and am the person identified as the successor attorney-in-fact for the principal. I hereby acknowledge that I accept my appointment as successor attorney-in-fact and that, in the absence of a specific provision to the contrary in the power of attorney, when I act as agent I shall exercise the powers for the benefit of the principal; I shall keep the assets of the principal separate from my assets; I shall exercise reasonable caution and prudence; and I shall keep a full and accurate record of all actions, receipts and disbursements on behalf of the principal.

_____   _____

Signature of Successor Attorney-in-Fact   Date

CHAPTER 6
Durable Unlimited Powers of Attorney for Financial Affairs

A *durable power of attorney* is a specific type of power of attorney that gives another person the authority to sign legal papers, transact business, buy or sell property, etc., and is only effective in one of two scenarios: (1) it may be written so that it *remains* in effect *even* if a person becomes disabled or incompetent, or (2) it may be written so that it *only* goes into effect *if and when* a person becomes disabled or incompetent. A durable power of attorney does not confer authority on another person to make health care decisions on someone else's behalf. Only a *durable health care power of attorney* can do that. There are two durable power of attorney forms contained in this book: one is written for the (1) scenario above (remains in effect if a person becomes incapacitated) and the other is written for the (2) scenario (it will only go into effect when and if a person becomes incapacitated). Note that a durable limited power of attorney for financial affairs is also possible to create for granting authority to act in specific situation or for particular transactions. However, because of its limited scope, this type of power of attorney is not as practical in situations when a durable power of attorney is generally used. If you wish to limit the powers that you grant in your durable power of attorney, please consult an attorney.

A *durable unlimited power of attorney for financial affairs* allows you to appoint an agent (who is then referred to as an 'attorney-in-fact') to handle your financial affairs during a period that you are unable to handle them yourself. With this form, you are giving another person the right to manage your financial and business matters on your behalf. They are given the power to act as you could, if you were able. If there is someone available who can be trusted implicitly to act on your behalf, the appointment of such a person can eliminate many problems that may arise if you are unable to handle your own affairs. The appointment of an agent for your financial affairs allows for the paying of bills, writing of checks, etc. while you are unable to do so yourself. You should appoint someone whom you trust completely. With the forms in this book, you are granting the appointed agent very broad powers to handle your affairs. You will give your agent the maximum power under law to perform any and all acts relating to any and all of your financial and/or business affairs Your attorney-in-fact (agent) is granted full power to act on your behalf in the same manner as if you were personally present.

The first durable unlimited power of attorney for financial affairs that is provided immediately appoints your chosen attorney-in-fact and provides that such appointment will remain in effect *even if* you become incapacitated. The second durable unlimited power of attorney for financial affairs that is provided will become effective *only* upon your incapacitation, as certified by your primary physician or, if your primary physician is not available, by any other attending physician. Neither power of attorney grants any power or authority to your designated attorney-in-fact regarding health care decisions. Only the *durable health care power of attorney* can confer those powers. You may, of course, choose to select the very same person to act as both your health care representative and your agent for financial affairs.

By accepting their appointment, your agent agrees to act in your best interest as he or she considers advisable. A durable unlimited power of attorney for financial matters may be revoked at any time and is automatically revoked on your death. The durable unlimited powers of attorney included in this chapter are intended to be used to confer a very powerful authority to another person. You will be providing another person with the power to handle all of your affairs (other than health care decisions). This is not a power that should be conferred lightly. Very serious thought should be given to both who you appoint as your attorney-in-fact (the person you authorize to act on your behalf) and to any specific directions that you may want to give to that person regarding financial decisions. You do not have to appoint anyone to handle your financial affairs, but it is often very useful to do so.

At the beginning of each of the documents are notices regarding the use of a durable power of attorney. They clearly explain the importance of caution in the use of this form and are applicable to all states. Please read each carefully to decide which of these forms are appropriate for your situation. Please note that this form provides a release for your attorney-in-fact to receive your medical records under the federal HIPAA regulations relating to the privacy of health care records. This does not confer any authority for your attorney-in-fact to make health care decisions on your behalf. The HIPAA release is for the purpose of allowing your attorney-in-fact to have access to your medical files for the purpose of paying or examining medical bills and charges.

Please also note that the state-specific advance health care directives that are explained in Chapter 10 *do not* contain a durable power of attorney for financial affairs. If you wish to have this type of document as part of your advance health care plans, you will need to complete one of the two types of forms that are contained in this chapter.

When You Should Use a Durable Power of Attorney for Financial Affairs

A *durable unlimited power of attorney* allows you to authorize someone to handle all of the following possible matters when you are incapacitated and unable to handle such matters yourself: real estate transactions; goods and services transactions; stock, bond, share and commodity transactions; banking transactions; business operating transactions; insurance transactions; estate transactions; legal claims and litigation; personal relationships and affairs; benefits from military service; records, reports and statements; retirement benefit transactions; making gifts to a spouse, children, parents and other descendants (if any); and tax matters.

A *durable unlimited power of attorney* provides that your agent will have total authority to act on your behalf for all financial and/or business matters (but not for health care decisions). If you wish to provide a very limited power to your agent, you may wish to use a *limited power of attorney* instead of a durable unlimited power of attorney. In addition, a durable unlimited power of attorney for financial affairs can *not* be used for health care decisions. You must use a *durable health care power of attorney* for that purpose.

Instructions for Durable Unlimited Power of Attorney for Financial Affairs (effective immediately)

(1) Goes into effect immediately and remains in effect even upon your Incapacitation

This form should be used only in situations where you desire to authorize another person to act for you in *all* transactions immediately and you wish the power to remain in effect in the event that you become incapacitated and unable to handle your own affairs. The grant of power under this document is unlimited (except for health care decisions). This form gives the person whom you designate as your "attorney-in-fact" broad powers to handle your property during your lifetime, which may include powers to mortgage, sell, or otherwise dispose of any real or personal property without advance notice to you or approval by you. This document does not authorize anyone to make medical or other health care decisions. You must execute a health care power of attorney to accomplish this. This form does provide a HIPPA medical records privacy release that will allow the person that you appoint to access any hospital or medical bills or records on you behalf. This form also provides that you will also name a successor attorney-in-fact who will have the same powers as the original person appointed, but who will only have the powers if the original person appointed is unable to perform the necessary tasks required by the power of attorney. The authority granted by this power of attorney may be revoked by you at any time and is automatically revoked if you die. If there is anything about this form that you do not understand, you should ask a lawyer to explain it to you. To complete this form, fill in the following:

(1) Name and address of person granting power (principal)
(2) Name and address of person granted power (attorney-in-fact)
(3) Name and address of successor to person originally granted power (successor attorney-in-fact) (optional-if not used, write N/A in this space)
(4) Printed name of principal, date of signature, and signature of principal (signed in front of notary public)
(5) Witnesses printed names and signatures (signed in front of notary public)
(6) Notary acknowledgement should be completed by the notary public
(7) Printed name and signature of attorney-in-fact and successor attorney-in-fact (need not be witnessed or notarized)
(8) Printed name and signature of attorney-in-fact and successor attorney-in-fact (optional-if not used, write N/A in this space) (need not be witnessed or notarized)

Durable Unlimited Power of Attorney For Financial Affairs

Effective Immediately

Notice to Adult Signing this Document: This is an important document. Before signing this document, you should know these important facts. By signing this document, you are not giving up any powers or rights to control your finances and property yourself. In addition to your own powers and rights, you are giving another person, your attorney-in-fact, broad powers to handle your finances and property, which may include powers to encumber, sell or otherwise dispose of any real or personal property without advance notice to you or approval by you. THE POWERS GRANTED UNDER THIS DOCUMENT ARE EFFECTIVE IMMEDIATELY AND WILL REMAIN IN EFFECT IF YOU BECOME DISABLED OR INCAPACITATED. This document does not authorize anyone to make medical or other health care decisions for you. If you own complex or special assets such as a business, or if there is anything about this form that you do not understand, you should ask a lawyer to explain this form to you before you sign it. If you wish to change your durable unlimited power of attorney, you must complete a new document and revoke this one. You have the right to revoke the designation of the attorney-in-fact and the right to revoke this entire document at any time and in any manner. You may revoke this document at any time by destroying it, by directing another person to destroy it in your presence or by signing a written and dated statement expressing your intent to revoke this document. If you revoke this document, you should notify your attorney-in-fact and any other person to whom you have given a copy of the form. You also should notify all parties having custody of your assets. These parties have no responsibility to you unless you actually notify them of the revocation. If your attorney-in-fact is your spouse and your marriage is annulled, or you are divorced after signing this document, this document may become invalid. Since some third parties or some transactions may not permit use of this document, it is advisable to check in advance, if possible, for any special requirements that may be imposed. You should sign this form only if the attorney-in- fact you name is reliable, trustworthy and competent to manage your affairs. Generally, you may designate any competent adult as the attorney-in-fact under this document.

① I, _____ (printed name),
of (address) _____, as
principal, ② do appoint _____ (printed name),
of (address) _____, as my
attorney-in- fact to act in my name, place and stead in any way which I myself could do, if I were personally present, with respect to all of the following matters to the extent that I am permitted by law to act through an agent: I grant my attorney-in-fact the maximum power under law to perform any act on my behalf that I could do personally, including but not limited to, all acts relating to any and all of my financial transactions and/or business affairs including all banking and financial institution transactions, all real estate or personal property transactions, all insurance

or annuity transactions, all claims and litigation, and any and all business transactions. **This power of attorney shall become effective immediately and shall remain in full effect upon my disability or incapacitation.** This power of attorney grants no power or authority regarding healthcare decisions to my designated attorney-in-fact.

③

If the attorney-in-fact named above is unable or unwilling to serve, then I appoint
_____(printed name),
of _____ (address),
to be my successor attorney-in-fact for all purposes hereunder.

My attorney-in-fact is granted full and unlimited power to act on my behalf in the same manner as if I were personally present. My attorney-in-fact accepts this appointment and agrees to act in my best interest as he or she considers advisable. To induce any third party to rely upon this power of attorney, I agree that any third party receiving a signed copy or facsimile of this power of attorney may rely upon such copy, and that revocation or termination of this power of attorney shall be ineffective as to such third party until actual notice or knowledge of such revocation or termination shall have been received by such third party. I, for myself and for my heirs, executors, legal representatives and assigns, agree to indemnify and hold harmless any such third party from any and all claims that may arise against such third party by reason of such third party having relied on the provisions of this power of attorney. This power of attorney may be revoked by me at any time and is automatically revoked upon my death. My attorney-in-fact shall not be compensated for his or her services nor shall my attorney-in-fact be liable to me, my estate, heirs, successors, or assigns for acting or refraining from acting under this document, except for willful misconduct or gross negligence. Revocation of this document is not effective unless a third party has actual knowledge of such revocation. I intend for my attorney-in-fact under this Power of Attorney to be treated as I would be with respect to my rights regarding the use and disclosure of my individually identifiable health information or other medical records. This release authority applies to any information governed by the Health Insurance Portability and Accountability Act of 1996 (aka HIPAA), 42 USC 1320d and 45 CFR 160-164.

④

Signature and Declaration of Principal

I, _____(printed name), the principal, sign my name to this power of attorney this _____day of _____and, being first duly sworn, do declare to the undersigned authority that I sign and execute this instrument as my power of attorney and that I sign it willingly, or willingly direct another to sign for me, that I execute it as my free and voluntary act for the purposes expressed in the power of attorney and that I am eighteen years of age or older, of sound mind and under no constraint or undue influence ,and that I have read and understand the contents of the notice at the beginning of this document.

_____
Signature of Principal

⑤ **Witness Attestation**

I, _____ (printed name), the first witness, and I, _____ (printed name), the second witness, sign my name to the foregoing power of attorney being first duly sworn and do declare to the undersigned authority that the principal signs and executes this instrument as his/her power of attorney and that he/she signs it willingly, or willingly directs another to sign for him/her, and that I, in the presence and hearing of the principal, sign this power of attorney as witness to the principal's signing and that to the best of my knowledge the principal is eighteen years of age or older, of sound mind and under no constraint or undue influence.

_____
Signature of First Witness

_____
Signature of Second Witness

⑥ Notary Acknowledgment

The State of _____

County of _____

Subscribed, sworn to and acknowledged before me by _____, the principal, and subscribed and sworn to before me by _____, the first witness, and _____, the second witness on this date _____.

_____

Notary Public Signature

Notary Public, In and for the County of _____ State of _____

My commission expires: _____   Notary Seal

⑦ Acknowledgment and Acceptance of Appointment as Attorney-in-Fact

I, _____, (printed name) have read the attached power of attorney and am the person identified as the attorney-in-fact for the principal. I hereby acknowledge that I accept my appointment as attorney-in-fact and that when I act as agent I shall exercise the powers for the benefit of the principal; I shall keep the assets of the principal separate from my assets; I shall exercise reasonable caution and prudence; and I shall keep a full and accurate record of all actions, receipts and disbursements on behalf of the principal.

_____   _____
Signature of Attorney-in-Fact   Date

⑧ Acknowledgment and Acceptance of Appointment as Successor Attorney-in-Fact

I, _____, (printed name) have read the attached power of attorney and am the person identified as the successor attorney-in-fact for the principal. I hereby acknowledge that I accept my appointment as successor attorney-in-fact and that, in the absence of a specific provision to the contrary in the power of attorney, when I act as agent I shall exercise the powers for the benefit of the principal; I shall keep the assets of the principal separate from my assets; I shall exercise reasonable caution and prudence; and I shall keep a full and accurate record of all actions, receipts and disbursements on behalf of the principal.

_____   _____
Signature of Successor Attorney-in-Fact   Date

Instructions for Durable Unlimited Power of Attorney for Financial Affairs (effective on incapacitation or disability)

(2) Goes into effect only upon your incapacitation as certified by your primary physician, or another physician, if your primary physician is not available.

This form should be used only in situations where you desire to authorize another person to act for you in *all* transactions but you desire that the powers granted will not take effect until you become incapacitated and unable to handle your own affairs. This documents also provides that your incapacitation must be certified by your primary physician, or another attending physician if your primary physician is not available. The grant of power under this document is unlimited (except for health care decisions). This form gives the person whom you designate as your "attorney-in-fact" broad powers to handle your property during your incapacitation, which may include powers to mortgage, sell, or otherwise dispose of any real or personal property without advance notice to you or approval by you. This document does not authorize anyone to make medical or other health care decisions. You must execute a durable health care power of attorney to accomplish this. This form does provide a HIPPA medical records privacy release that will allow the person that you appoint to access any hospital or medical bills or records on you behalf. This form also provides that you will also name a successor attorney-in-fact who will have the same powers as the original person appointed, but who will only have the powers if the original person appointed is unable to perform the necessary tasks required by the power of attorney. The authority granted by this power of attorney may be revoked by you at any time and is automatically revoked if you die. If there is anything about this form that you do not understand, you should ask a lawyer to explain it to you. Please note that this form provides a release for your attorney-in-fact to receive your medical records under the federal HIPAA regulations relating to the privacy of health care records.

To complete this form, fill in the following:

① Name and address of person granting power (principal)
② Name and address of person granted power (attorney-in-fact)
③ Name and address of successor to person originally granted power (successor attorney-in-fact) (optional-if not used, write N/A in this space)
④ Printed name of principal, date of signature, and signature of principal (signed in front of notary public)
⑤ Witnesses printed names and signatures (signed in front of notary public)
⑥ Notary acknowledgement should be completed by the notary public
⑦ Printed name and signature of attorney-in-fact and successor attorney-in-fact (need not be witnessed or notarized)
⑧ Printed name and signature of attorney-in-fact and successor attorney-in-fact (optional-if not used, write N/A in this space) (need not be witnessed or notarized)

Durable Unlimited Power of Attorney For Financial Affairs

Effective Only Upon Incapacitation or Disability

Notice to Adult Signing this Document: This is an important document. Before signing this document, you should know these important facts. By signing this document, you are not giving up any powers or rights to control your finances and property yourself. In addition to your own powers and rights, you are giving another person, your attorney-in-fact, broad powers to handle your finances and property, which may include powers to encumber, sell or otherwise dispose of any real or personal property without advance notice to you or approval by you. THE POWERS GRANTED UNDER THIS DOCUMENT WILL ONLY GO INTO EFFECT IF YOU BECOME DISABLED OR INCAPACITATED, AS CERTIFIED BY YOUR PRIMARY PHYSICIAN, OR BY ANOTHER ATTENDING PHYSICIAN, IF YOUR PRIMARY PHYSICIAN IS NOT AVAILABLE. This document does not authorize anyone to make medical or other health care decisions for you. If you own complex or special assets such as a business, or if there is anything about this form that you do not understand, you should ask a lawyer to explain this form to you before you sign it. If you wish to change your durable unlimited power of attorney, you must complete a new document and revoke this one. You have the right to revoke the designation of the attorney-in-fact and the right to revoke this entire document at any time and in any manner. You may revoke this document at any time by destroying it, by directing another person to destroy it in your presence or by signing a written and dated statement expressing your intent to revoke this document. If you revoke this document, you should notify your attorney-in-fact and any other person to whom you have given a copy of the form. You also should notify all parties having custody of your assets. These parties have no responsibility to you unless you actually notify them of the revocation. If your attorney-in-fact is your spouse and your marriage is annulled, or you are divorced after signing this document, this document may become invalid. Since some third parties or some transactions may not permit use of this document, it is advisable to check in advance, if possible, for any special requirements that may be imposed. You should sign this form only if the attorney-in-fact you name is reliable, trustworthy and competent to manage your affairs. Generally, you may designate any competent adult as the attorney-in-fact under this document.

① I, _____ (printed name),
of (address) _____ , as principal,
② do appoint _____ (printed name),
of (address) _____ , as my
attorney-in-fact to act in my name, place and stead in any way which I myself could do, if I were personally present, with respect to all of the following matters to the extent that I am permitted by law to act through an agent: I grant my attorney-in-fact the maximum power under law to perform any act on my behalf that I could do personally, including but not limited to, all acts relating to any and all of my financial transactions and/or business affairs including all banking and financial institution transactions, all real estate or personal property transactions, all insurance or annuity

transactions, all claims and litigation, and any and all business transactions. This power of attorney shall only become effective upon my disability or incapacitation, as certified by my primary physician, or if my primary physician is not available, by any other attending physician. This power of attorney grants no power or authority regarding healthcare decisions to my designated attorney-in-fact.

③

If the attorney-in-fact named above is unable or unwilling to serve, then I appoint

_____(printed name),

of_____ (address),

to be my successor attorney-in-fact for all purposes hereunder.

My attorney-in-fact is granted full and unlimited power to act on my behalf in the same manner as if I were personally present. My attorney-in-fact accepts this appointment and agrees to act in my best interest as he or she considers advisable. To induce any third party to rely upon this power of attorney, I agree that any third party receiving a signed copy or facsimile of this power of attorney may rely upon such copy, and that revocation or termination of this power of attorney shall be ineffective as to such third party until actual notice or knowledge of such revocation or termination shall have been received by such third party. I, for myself and for my heirs, executors, legal representatives and assigns, agree to indemnify and hold harmless any such third party from any and all claims that may arise against such third party by reason of such third party having relied on the provisions of this power of attorney. This power of attorney may be revoked by me at any time and is automatically revoked upon my death. My attorney-in-fact shall not be compensated for his or her services nor shall my attorney-in-fact be liable to me, my estate, heirs, successors, or assigns for acting or refraining from acting under this document, except for willful misconduct or gross negligence. Revocation of this document is not effective unless a third party has actual knowledge of such revocation.

I intend for my attorney-in-fact under this Power of Attorney to be treated as I would be with respect to my rights regarding the use and disclosure of my individually identifiable health information or other medical records. This release authority applies to any information governed by the Health Insurance Portability and Accountability Act of 1996 (aka HIPAA), 42 USC 1320d and 45 CFR 160-164.

④

Signature and Declaration of Principal

I, _____ (printed name), the principal, sign my name to this power of attorney this _____day of _____and, being first duly sworn, do declare to the undersigned authority that I sign and execute this instrument as my power of attorney and that I sign it willingly, or willingly direct another to sign for me, that I execute it as my free and voluntary act for the purposes expressed in the power of attorney and that I am eighteen years of age or older, of sound mind and under no constraint or undue influence ,and that I have read and understand the contents of the notice at the beginning of this document.

_____

Signature of Principal

⑤ Witness Attestation

I, _____ (printed name), the first witness, and I, _____ (printed name), the second witness, sign my name to the foregoing power of attorney being first duly sworn and do declare to the undersigned authority that the principal signs and executes this instrument as his/her power of attorney and that he/she signs it willingly, or willingly directs another to sign for him/her, and that I, in the presence and hearing of the principal, sign this power of attorney as witness to the principal's signing and that to the best of my knowledge the principal is eighteen years of age or older, of sound mind and under no constraint or undue influence.

_____   _____
Signature of First Witness   Signature of Second Witness

⑥ Notary Acknowledgment

The State of _____

County of _____

Subscribed, sworn to and acknowledged before me by _____,the principal, and subscribed and sworn to before me by _____, the first witness, and _____,the second witness on this date _____.

_____
Notary Public Signature
Notary Public, In and for the County of _____ State of _____
My commission expires: _____ Notary Seal

⑦ Acknowledgment and Acceptance of Appointment as Attorney-in-Fact

I, _____ (printed name) have read the attached power of attorney and am the person identified as the attorney-in-fact for the principal. I hereby acknowledge that I accept my appointment as attorney-in-fact and that when I act as agent I shall exercise the powers for the benefit of the principal; I shall keep the assets of the principal separate from my assets; I shall exercise reasonable caution and prudence; and I shall keep a full and accurate record of all actions, receipts and disbursements on behalf of the principal.

_____   _____
Signature of Attorney-in-Fact   Date

⑧ Acknowledgment and Acceptance of Appointment as Successor Attorney-in-Fact

I, _____ (printed name) have read the attached power of attorney and am the person identified as the successor attorney-in-fact for the principal. I hereby acknowledge that I accept my appointment as successor attorney-in-fact and that, in the absence of a specific provision to the contrary in the power of attorney, when I act as agent I shall exercise the powers for the benefit of the principal; I shall keep the assets of the principal separate from my assets; I shall exercise reasonable caution and prudence; and I shall keep a full and accurate record of all actions, receipts and disbursements on behalf of the principal.

_____   _____
Signature of Successor Attorney-in-Fact   Date

CHAPTER 7
Durable Health Care Power of Attorney

A *power of attorney* is a document that is used to allow one person to give authority to another person to act on their behalf. The person signing the power of attorney grants legal authority to another to "stand in their shoes" and act legally for them. The person who receives the power of attorney is called an *attorney-in-fact*. This title and the power of attorney form does not mean that the person receiving the power has to be a lawyer. Power of attorney forms are useful documents for many occasions. They can be used to authorize someone else to sign certain documents if you can not be present when the signatures are necessary. Traditionally, financial and property matters were the type of actions handled with powers of attorney. Increasingly, however, people are using a specific type of power of attorney to authorize other persons to make health care decisions on their behalf in the event of a disability which makes the person unable to communicate their wishes to doctors or other health care providers. This broad type of power of attorney is called a *durable health care power of attorney*. It is different from *durable power of attorney for financial affairs*, which gives another person the authority to sign legal papers, transact business, buy or sell property, etc. but is intended to remain in effect even if a person becomes disabled or incompetent. A *durable power of attorney for financial affairs* does not confer authority on another person to make health care decisions on someone else's behalf. Only a *durable health care power of attorney* can do that.

When You Should Use a Durable Health Care Power of Attorney

Durable health care powers of attorney are useful documents that go beyond the provisions of a living will. They provide for health care options that living wills do not cover, and are important additions to the use of a living will. Basically, a durable health care power of attorney allows you to appoint someone to act for you in making health care decisions when you are unable to make them for yourself. A living will does not provide for this. Also, a durable health care power of attorney generally applies to all medical decisions (unless you specifically limit the power). Most living wills only apply to certain decisions regarding life support at the end of your life and are most useful in "terminal illness" or "permanent unconsciousness" situations.

Additionally, a durable health care power of attorney can provide your chosen agent with a valuable flexibility in making decisions regarding medical choices that may arise. Often, during the course of medical treatment, unforeseen situations may occur that require immediate decision-making. If you are unable to communicate your desires regarding such choices, the appointment of a *health care representative* for you (appointed with a durable health care power of attorney) will allow such decisions to be made on your behalf by a trusted person.

Finally, a durable health care power of attorney can provide specific detailed instructions regarding what you would like done by your attending physician in specific circumstances. Generally, living wills are limited to options for the withholding of life support. In order to be certain that you have made provisions for most potential health care situations, it is recommended you prepare both a living will and a durable health care power of attorney. Not everyone, however, has a trusted person available to serve as their health care representative. In these situations, the use of a living will alone will be necessary. It is, of course, possible to add additional instructions to any living will to clearly and specifically indicate your desires. (Note: state-specific living wills are contained in the state-specific advance health care directives that are explained in Chapter 10 and contained on the enclosed CD).

Your health care representative can be a relative or close friend. It should be someone who knows you very well and whom you trust completely. Your representative should be someone who is not afraid to ask questions of health care providers and is able to make difficult decisions. Your representative may need to be assertive on your behalf. You should discuss your choice with your representative and make certain that he or she understands the responsibilities involved.

All states have enacted legislation regarding this type of form and recognize the validity of this type of legal document. In some states, they are called Appointment of Health Care Agent; in others, they are referred to as a Health Care Proxy. The form included in this book is officially titled Durable Health Care Power of Attorney and Appointment of Health Care Agent and Proxy, and is designed to be legally valid in all states. Information regarding each state's provisions are included in the Appendix.

The durable health care power of attorney included in this chapter is intended to be used to confer a very powerful authority to another person. In some cases, this may actually mean that you are giving that other person the power of life or death over you. This is not a power that should be conferred lightly. Very serious thought should be given to both who you appoint as your health care attorney-in-fact (the person you authorize to act on your behalf) and to any specific directions that you may want to give to that person regarding health care decisions. You may, of course, revoke your durable health care power of attorney at any time prior to your incapacitation (and even during any incapacitation if you are able to make your desire to revoke the power known). Remember, however, that should you become disabled or incapacitated and unable to communicate your wishes to anyone, you may be unable to communicate your desire to revoke your durable health care power of attorney.

Please note that this form provides a release for your health care representative to receive your medical records under the federal HIPAA regulations relating to the privacy of health care records. Also, at the beginning of the form is a notice that clearly explains the importance of caution in the use of this form and is applicable to all states. Please read it carefully before you sign your durable health care power of attorney.

This chapter contains a general, standardized durable health care power of attorney. Chapter 10 contains state-specific health care powers of attorney as part of the state-specific advance health care directives that have been taken directly from the most recent legislation regarding health care powers of attorney in each state. A few states do not currently have specific legislation providing express statutory recognition of health care powers of attorney. For those states, the durable health care power of attorney in this chapter has been prepared by legal professionals to comply with the basic requirements that courts in that state or other states have found important. In such states, be assured that courts, health care professionals, and physicians will be guided by this expression of your desires concerning life support as expressed in the durable health care power of attorney prepared using this book. You may use either the general durable health care power of attorney form or the state-specific advance health care directive form for your state. Please compare your state's form (in your state's advance health care directive in Chapter 10) with the standardized form in this chapter and select the appropriate form that you feel best expresses your wishes regarding the appointment of a health care agent to make your health care decisions for you if you are unable to make those decisions for yourself.

The Federal Patient Self-Determination Act encourages all people to make their own decisions about the type of medical care they wish to receive. This act also requires all health care agencies (hospitals, long-term care facilities, and home health agencies) receiving Medicare and Medicaid reimbursement to recognize a living will and/or health care power of attorney as advance directives. Under this Act, all health care agencies must ask you if you have advance directives and must give you materials with information about your rights under state law. The durable health care power of attorney included in this chapter and/or the state-specific health care power of attorney included in the state-specific advance health care directives in Chapter 10 must be recognized by all health care agencies.

Revoking Your Durable Health Care Power of Attorney

All states have provided methods for the easy revocation of durable health care powers of attorney. Since such forms provide authority to medical personnel to withhold life-support technology that will likely result in death to the patient, great care must be taken to insure that a change of mind by the patient is heeded. For the revocation of a durable power of attorney for health care, any one of the following methods of revocation is generally acceptable:

- Physical destruction of the durable power of attorney for health care, such as tearing, burning, or mutilating the document.

- A written revocation of the durable power of attorney for health care by you or by a person acting at your direction. A form for this is provided later in this chapter and on the CD.

- An oral revocation in the presence of a witness who signs and dates an affidavit confirming a revocation. This oral declaration may take in any manner (verbal or non-verbal). Most states allow for a person to revoke such a document by any indication (even non-verbal) of the intent to revoke a durable power of attorney for health care, regardless of his or her physical or mental condition. A form for this (Witness Affidavit of Oral Revocation of Durable Health Care Power of Attorney) is included later in this chapter and on the CD.

If you use the revocation forms in this chapter or if you physically destroy your health care power of attorney, make sure that you provide a copy (or notice) of this revocation to anyone or any health care facility that has a copy or original of the durable power of attorney for health care that you are revoking.

Instructions for Durable Health Care Power of Attorney

This form should be used for preparing a durable health care power of attorney that appoints another person whom you chose to have the authority to make health care decisions for you in the event that you become incapacitated.

To complete this form, you will need the following information:

(1) Name and address of person granting power of attorney

(2) Name and address of person appointed as the "health care representative" (same as the "attorney-in-fact for health care decisions")

(3) State whose laws will govern the powers granted

(4) Signature of person granting power of attorney. IMPORTANT NOTE: You should only sign this section if you have carefully read and agree with the statement that grants your health care representative the authority to order the withholding of nutrition, hydration, and any other medical care when you are diagnosed as being in a persistent vegetative state.

(5) Any additional terms or conditions that you wish to add

(6) Date of signing of durable health care power of attorney

(7) Your signature and printed name (do not sign unless in front of a notary public and witnesses)

(8) Signature and printed name of witnesses (signed in front of a notary)

(9) The notary acknowledgment section (to be completed by notary public)

(10) Signature and printed name of person appointed as health care representative (This signature need not be witnessed or notarized)

Durable Health Care Power of Attorney and Appointment of Health Care Agent and Proxy

NOTICE TO ADULT SIGNING THIS DOCUMENT: This is an important legal document. Before executing this document, you should know these facts: This document gives the person you designate (the attorney-in-fact) the power to make MOST health care decisions for you if you lose the capacity to make informed health care decisions for yourself. This power is effective only when your attending physician determines that you have lost the capacity to make informed health care decisions for yourself. Regardless of this document, as long as you have the capacity to make informed health care decisions for yourself, you retain the right to make all medical and other health care decisions for yourself. You may include specific limitations in this document on the authority of the attorney-in-fact to make health care decisions for you. Subject to any specific limitations you include in this document, if your attending physician determines that you have lost the capacity to make an informed decision on a health care matter, the attorney-in-fact GENERALLY will be authorized by this document to make health care decisions for you to the same extent as you could make those decisions yourself, if you had the capacity to do so. The authority of the attorney-in-fact to make health care decisions for you GENERALLY will include the authority to give informed consent, to refuse to give informed consent, or to withdraw informed consent to any care, treatment, service, or procedure to maintain, diagnose, or treat a physical or mental condition. Additionally, when exercising authority to make health care decisions for you, the attorney-in-fact will have to act consistently with your desires or, if your desires are unknown, to act in your best interest. You may express your desires to the attorney-in-fact by including them in this document or by making them known to the attorney-in-fact in another manner. When acting pursuant to this document, the attorney-in-fact GENERALLY will have the same rights that you have to receive information about proposed health care, to review health care records, and to consent to the disclosure of health care records. You can limit that right in this document if you so choose. GENERALLY, you may designate any competent adult as the attorney-in-fact under this document. You have the right to revoke the designation of the attorney-in-fact and the right to revoke this entire document at any time and in any manner. Any such revocation generally will be effective when you express your intention to make the revocation. However, if you made your attending physician aware of this document, any such revocation will be effective only when you communicate it to your attending physician, or when a witness to the revocation or other health care personnel to whom the revocation is communicated by such a witness communicates it to your attending physician. If you execute this document and create a valid Health Care Power of Attorney with it, this will revoke any prior, valid power of attorney for health care that you created, unless you indicate otherwise in this document. This document is not valid as a Health Care Power of Attorney unless it is acknowledged before a notary public or is signed by at least two adult witnesses who are present when you sign or acknowledge your signature. No person who is related to you by blood, marriage, or adoption may be a witness. The attorney-in-fact, your attending physician, and the administrator of any nursing home in which you are receiving care also are ineligible to be witnesses. If there is anything in this document that you do not understand, you should ask a lawyer to explain it to you.

① I, _____ (printed name) , residing at _____, appoint the following person as my attorney-in-fact for health care decisions, my health care agent, and confer upon this person my health care proxy. This person shall hereafter referred to as my "health care representative":
② _____ (printed name) , residing at _____.

③ I grant my health care representative the maximum power under law to perform any acts on my behalf regarding health care matters that I could do personally under the laws of the State of _____, including specifically the power to make any health decisions on my behalf, upon the terms and conditions set forth below. My health care representative accepts this appointment and agrees to act in my best interest as he or she considers advisable. This health care power of attorney and appointment of health care agent and proxy may be revoked by me at any time and is automatically revoked on my death. However, this power of attorney shall not be affected by my present or future disability or incapacity.

This health care power of attorney and appointment of health care agent and proxy has the following terms and conditions:

If I have signed a Living Will or Directive to Physicians, and it is still in effect, I direct that my health care representative abide by the directions that I have set out in that document. If at any time I should have an incurable injury, disease, or illness which has been certified as a terminal condition by my attending physician and one additional physician, both of whom have personally examined me, and such physicians have determined that there can be no recovery from such condition and my death is imminent, and where the application of life prolonging procedures would serve only to artificially prolong the dying process, then:

I direct my health care representative to assure that such procedures be withheld or withdrawn, and that I be permitted to die naturally with only the administration of medication, the administration of nutrition and/or hydration, or the performance of any medical procedure deemed necessary to provide me with comfort, care, or to alleviate pain. If at any time I should have been diagnosed as being in a persistent vegetative state which has been certified as incurable by my attending physician and one additional physician, both of whom have personally examined me, and such physicians have determined that there can be no recovery from such condition, and where the application of life prolonging procedures would serve only to artificially prolong the dying process, then: I direct that my health care representative assure that such procedures be withheld or withdrawn, and that I be permitted to die naturally with only the administration of medication, the administration of nutrition and/or hydration, or the performance of any medical procedure deemed necessary to provide me with comfort, care, or to alleviate pain.

④ THE FOLLOWING INSTRUCTIONS (IN BOLDFACE TYPE) ONLY APPLY IF I HAVE SIGNED MY NAME IN THIS SPACE: _____

However, if at any time I should have been diagnosed as being in a persistent vegetative state which has been certified as incurable by my attending physician and one additional physician, both of whom have personally examined me, and such physicians have determined that there can be no recovery from such condition, I also direct that my health care representative have sole authority to order the withholding of any aid, including the administration of nutrition, hydration, and any other medical procedure deemed necessary to provide me with comfort, care, or to alleviate pain.

If I am able to communicate in any manner, including even blinking my eyes, I direct that my health care representative try and discuss with me the specifics of any proposed health care decision.

⑤ If I have any further terms or conditions, I state them here:

I have discussed my health care wishes with the person whom I have herein appointed as my health care representative, I am fully satisfied that the person who I have herein appointed as my health care representative will know my wishes with respect to my health care and I have full faith and confidence in their good judgement.

I further direct that my health care representative shall have full authority to do the following, should I lack the capacity to make such a decision myself, provided however, that this listing shall in no way limit the full authority that I give my health care representative to make health care decisions on my behalf:

a. to give informed consent to any health care procedure;

b. to sign any documents necessary to carry out or withhold any health care procedures on my behalf, including any waivers or releases of liabilities required by any health care provider;

c. to give or withhold consent for any health care or treatment;

d. to revoke or change any consent previously given or implied by law for any health care treatment;

e. to arrange for or authorize my placement or removal from any health care facility or institution;

f. to require that any procedures be discontinued, including the withholding of any medical treatment and/or aid, including the administration of nutrition, hydration, and any other medical procedure deemed necessary to provide me with comfort, care, or to alleviate pain, subject to the conditions earlier provided in this document;

g. to authorize the administration of pain-relieving drugs, even if they may shorten my life.

I desire that my wishes with respect to all health care matters be carried out through the authority that I have herein provided to my health care representative, despite any contrary wishes, beliefs, or opinions of any members of my family, relatives, or friends. I have read the Notice that precedes this document. I understand the full importance of this appointment, and I am emotionally and mentally competent to make this appointment of health care representative. I intend for my health care representative to be treated as I would be with respect to my rights regarding the use and disclosure of my individually identifiable health information or other medical records. This release authority applies to any information governed by the Health Insurance Portability and Accountability Act of 1996 (aka HIPAA), 42 USC 1320d and 45 CFR 160-164.

I declare to the undersigned authority that I sign and execute this instrument as my health care power of attorney and that I sign it willingly, or willingly direct another to sign for me, that I execute it as my free and voluntary act for the purposes expressed in this document and that I am nineteen years of age or older, of sound mind and under no constraint or undue influence ,and that I have read and understand the contents of the notice at the beginning of this document, and .that I understand the purpose and effect of this document.

⑥ Dated _____ , 20_____

⑦ _____
Signature of person granting health care power of attorney and appointing health care representative

_____
Printed name of person granting health care power of attorney and appointing health care representative

⑧ **Witness Attestation**

I, _____(printed name), the first witness,
and I, _____(printed name), the
second witness, sign my name to the foregoing power of attorney being first duly sworn and do declare to the undersigned authority that the principal signs and executes this instrument as his/her power of attorney and that he/she signs it willingly, or willingly directs another to sign for him/her, and that I, in the presence and hearing of the principal, sign this power of attorney as witness to the principal's signing and that to the best of my knowledge the principal is nineteen years of age or older, of sound mind and under no constraint or undue influence. I am nineteen years of age or older. I am not appointed as the health care representative or attorney-in-fact by this document. I am not related to the principal by blood, adoption or marriage, nor am I entitled to any portion of the principal's estate under the laws of intestate succession or under any will or codicil of the principal. I also do not provide health care services to the principal, nor an employee of any health care facility in which the principal is a patient and am not financially responsible for the principal's health care.

_____   _____
Signature of First Witness   Address of First Witness

_____   _____
Signature of Second Witness   Address of Second Witness

⑨ Notary Acknowledgment

State of _____   County of _____

Subscribed, sworn to and acknowledged before me on this date _____ , 20_____ by
_____, the principal, who came before me personally, and under oath, stated that he or she is the person described in the above document and he or she signed the above document in my presence, or willingly directed another to sign for him or her. I declare under penalty of perjury that the person whose name is subscribed to this instrument appears to be of sound mind and under no duress, fraud, or undue influence. This document was also subscribed and sworn to before me on this date by _____, the first witness, and _____,the second witness .

_____

Notary Signature
Notary Public
In and for the County of _____   State of _____
My commission expires: _____   Notary Seal

In California, Delaware, Georgia, and Vermont, the following statement is required to be signed by a patient advocate, ombudsman (in California, Delaware and Vermont) or facility director (in Georgia or Vermont, if the principal is a patient in a skilled nursing facility:

Statement of Patient Advocate or Ombudsman: I declare under penalty of perjury under the laws of the State of _____ that I am a patient advocate or ombudsman (or medical facility director) and am serving as a witness required by the laws of this state and that the principal appeared to be of sound mind and under no duress, fraud, or undue influence.
Dated _____

_____   _____
Signature of Patient Advocate or Ombudsman   Printed name and title of witness

Acceptance of Appointment as Health Care Attorney-in-Fact and Health Care Representative

I have read the attached durable health care power of attorney and am the person identified as the attorney-in-fact and health care representative for the principal. I hereby acknowledge that I accept my appointment as health care attorney-in-fact and health care representative and that when I act as agent I shall exercise the powers in the best interests of the principal.

⑩_____
Signature of person granted health care power of attorney and appointed as health care representative

_____
Printed name of person granted health care power of attorney and appointed as health care representative

Instructions for Revocation of a Durable Health Care Power of Attorney

On the following page, there is included a revocation of health care power of attorney. You have the right at any time to revoke your health care power of attorney. Remember, however, that should you become disabled or incapacitated and unable to communicate your wishes to anyone, you may be unable to communicate your desire to revoke your health care power of attorney. In any event, if you choose to revoke your health care power of attorney, a copy of this revocation should be provided to the person to whom the power was originally given. Copies should also be given to any party that may have had dealings with the attorney-in-fact before the revocation and to any party with whom the attorney-in-fact may be expected to attempt to deal with after the revocation, for example, your family physician.

Also note that you may also revoke a health care power of attorney by an oral revocation that takes place in the presence of a witness who then signs and date a written statement that confirms the revocation. Your oral declaration may take any manner, even a non-verbal indication (such as nodding your head or blinking your eyes) that signifies your intent to revoke the health care power of attorney. Such revocation can take place regardless of your physical or mental condition, as long as you are able to communicate, in some recognizable manner, your clear intent to revoke the power that was granted. For an oral revocation, use the Witness Affidavit of Oral Revocation of Durable Health Care Power of Attorney.

If you are able to, this form should be filled out and signed by the person revoking the health care power of attorney. It should also be notarized.

① Name and address of person granting original health care power of attorney
② Date of original durable health care power of attorney (that is now being revoked)
③ Name and address of person originally appointed as the "health care representative"
④ Date of signing of Revocation of Durable Health Care Power of Attorney
⑤ Your signature and printed name

Revocation of Durable Health Care Power of Attorney

① I, _____ (printed name),
  of (address) _____
② do revoke the Durable Health Care Power of Attorney dated _____ , 20_____ ,
③ which was granted to _____ (printed name),
  of (address) _____ ,
  to act as my attorney-in-fact for health care decisions and I revoke any appointment of the above
  person as my health care agent, health care representative, or health care proxy.

④ Dated _____ , 20_____

⑤ _____
Signature of person revoking power of attorney

_____
Printed name of person revoking power of attorney

Instructions for Witness Affidavit of Oral Revocation of Durable Health Care Power of Attorney

If it is necessary to use the Witness Affidavit of Oral Revocation of Durable Health Care Power Of Attorney form, the witness should actually observe your indication of an intention to revoke your durable health care power of attorney. This may take the form of any verbal or non-verbal direction, as long as your intent to revoke is clearly and unmistakably evident to the witness. This form does not need to be notarized to be effective. Make sure that you provide a copy of this revocation to anyone or any health care facility that has a copy or original of the durable health care power of attorney that you are revoking.

To complete this document, fill in the following information:

① Name and address of person who originally signed health care power of attorney (principal)
② Date of original health care power of attorney
③ State in which health care power of attorney was originally signed
④ Printed name of witness to act of revocation
⑤ Date of act of revocation
⑥ Witness signature
⑦ Date of witness signature
⑧ Printed name of witness

Witness Affidavit of Oral Revocation of Durable Health Care Power of Attorney

The following person ① _____,
referred to as the Principal, was the maker and signatory of a Durable Health Care Power of Attorney which was dated ② _____ , and which was executed by him or her for use in the State of ③ _____ .

By this written affidavit, I, ④ _____ , the witness, hereby affirm that on the date of ⑤ _____ , I personally witnessed the above-named declarant make known to me, through verbal and/or non-verbal methods, their clear and unmistakable intent to entirely revoke such Durable Health Care Power of Attorney, or any other appointment or designation of a person to make any health care decisions on his or her behalf. It is my belief that the above-named principal fully intended that all of the above-mentioned documents no longer have any force or effect whatsoever.

Witness Acknowledgment

The declarant is personally known to me and I believe him or her to be of sound mind and under no duress, fraud, or undue influence.

Witness Signature ⑥ _____   Date ⑦ _____

Printed Name of Witness ⑧ _____

CHAPTER 8
Revocation of Powers of Attorney

This document may be used with any of the previous power of attorney forms. The revocation is used to terminate the original authority that was granted to the other person in the first place. Some limited powers of attorney specifiy that the powers that are granted will end on a specific date. If that is the case, you will not need a revocation unless you wish the powers to end sooner than the date specified. If the grant of power was for a limited purpose and that purpose is complete but no date for the power to end was specified, this revocation should be used as soon after the transaction as possible. In any event, if you choose to revoke a power of attorney, a copy of this revocation should be provided to the person to whom the power was given. Copies should also be given to any party that may have had dealings with the attorney-in-fact before the revocation and to any party with whom the attorney-in-fact may be expected to attempt to deal with after the revocation. If you feel that it is important to verify the revocation of your power of attorney, you should have any third party that you supply with a copy of the revocation sign another copy for you to keep. If that is not possible, you should mail a copy of the revocation to that person or institution by first class mail, with a return receipt requested that requires a signature to verify delivery.

Although this revocation may be used to revoke a health care power of attorney, please also note that there are other acceptable methods to revoke a health care power of attorney. These are noted in Chapter 7.

To complete this document, fill in the following information:

① Printed name and address of person who originally granted power (principal)
② Date of original power of attorney
③ Printed name and address of person granted power (attorney-in-fact)
④ Date of revocation of power of attorney
⑤ Signature of person revoking power of attorney (principal) (signed in front of notary)
⑥ Notary to complete the notary acknowledgement

Revocation of Power of Attorney

① I, _____ (printed name) ,
address: _____

② do revoke the power of attorney dated _____ , 20 _____ ,
③ which was granted to _____ (printed name),
address:_____ ,

to act as my attorney-in-fact.

④ This Revocation is dated _____ , 20 _____

⑤ _____
Signature of Person Revoking Power of Attorney

⑥ **Notary Acknowledgement**

State of _____
County of _____

On _____ , 20 _____ , _____ personally
came before me and, being duly sworn, did state that he or she is the person described in the
above document and that he or she signed the above document in my presence.

_____
Signature of Notary Public

Notary Public, In and for the County of _____
State of _____

My commission expires: _____   Notary Seal

CHAPTER 9
State-Specific Durable Powers of Attorney

Although, the forms provided in Chapter 6 of this book (durable unlimited powers of attorney for financial affairs) are legally-valid in all states, some states provide their own particular form for a durable power of attorney. you may choose to use one of the generic forms provided in Chapter 6 or you may choose to use the state-specific forms provided in this chapter.

A '*state-specific statutory form*' is a form that has been taken directly from the laws of your particular state. The legal effects of the language in such a document have been approved by the legislature of the state. This provides an advantage in that the legal language in such a 'statutory' form is generally familiar to most financial institutions in the particular state and they know that such language has been approved. This does not mean, however, that other 'non-statutory' forms are not legally valid in the state as well. All states specifically provide, in their legislation regarding powers of attorney, that power of attorney forms other than those contained in the statute itself are legally valid. Anyone may use a 'non-statutory' legal form, such as those in Chapters 3 through 7, with language that they find appropriate to their own situation, as long as the document meets certain minimum legal standards for a particular state. All of the forms in this book meet such required legal standards. The following states have developed state-specific statutory forms for durable powers of attorney:

Alaska, Arkansas, California, Colorado, Connecticut, District of Columbia, Georgia, Illinois, Montana, Nebraska, New Hampshire, New Mexico, New York, North Carolina, Oklahoma, Pennsylvania, Rhode Island, Texas

In all other states, the legislatures have not developed specific forms for durable powers of attorney. In such situations, you may use the individual durable unlimited power of attorney forms provided in Chapter 6. The forms in Chapter 6 have been prepared following any guidelines or requirements set out by the particular state's legislature.

When You Should Use a State-Specific Durable Power of Attorney

You should use the form in this chapter for your specific state if, after reading through the form, you feel that it meets your particular needs. The forms in this chapter have been taken directly from each state's statutes and, thus, are well known to financial institutions in the particular state. This makes these forms more readily acceptable to some institutions. However, if the forms in this chapter do not fit your particular needs, you should read through the two durable power of attorney forms in Chapter 6 and determine if either of those forms will be more acceptable in your situation. If so, you may use the form in Chapter 6.

Alaska Durable Power of Attorney

THE POWERS GRANTED FROM THE PRINCIPAL TO THE AGENT OR AGENTS IN THE FOLLOWING DOCUMENT ARE VERY BROAD. THEY MAY INCLUDE THE POWER TO DISPOSE, SELL, CONVEY, AND ENCUMBER YOUR REAL AND PERSONAL PROPERTY, AND THE POWER TO MAKE YOUR HEALTH CARE DECISIONS. ACCORDINGLY, THE FOLLOWING DOCUMENT SHOULD ONLY BE USED AFTER CAREFUL CONSIDERATION. IF YOU HAVE ANY QUESTIONS ABOUT THIS DOCUMENT, YOU SHOULD SEEK COMPETENT ADVICE. YOU MAY REVOKE THIS POWER OF ATTORNEY AT ANY TIME.

Pursuant to AS 13.26.338 - 13.26.353,

I, _____(Name of principal)

of _____(Address of principal),

do hereby appoint _____

_____

(Name and address of agent or agents), my attorney(s)-in-fact to act as I have checked below in my name, place, and stead in any way which I myself could do, if I were personally present, with respect to the following matters, as each of them is defined in AS 13.26.344 , to the full extent that I am permitted by law to act through an agent:

THE AGENT OR AGENTS YOU HAVE APPOINTED WILL HAVE ALL THE POWERS LISTED BELOW UNLESS YOU DRAW A LINE THROUGH A CATEGORY; AND INITIAL THE BOX OPPOSITE THAT CATEGORY

(A) real estate transactions   (   )
(B) transactions involving tangible personal property, chattels, and goods   (   )
(C) bonds, shares, and commodities transactions   (   )
(D) banking transactions   (   )
(E) business operating transactions   (   )
(F) insurance transactions   (   )
(G) estate transactions   (   )
(H) gift transactions   (   )
(I) claims and litigation   (   )
(J) personal relationships and affairs   (   )
(K) benefits from government programs and military service   (   )
(L) records, reports, and statements   (   )
(M) delegation   (   )
(N) all other matters, including those specified as follows: (   )

IF YOU HAVE APPOINTED MORE THAN ONE AGENT, CHECK ONE OF THE FOLLOWING:

( ) Each agent may exercise the powers conferred separately, without the consent of any other agent.

( ) All agents shall exercise the powers conferred jointly, with the consent of all other agents.

TO INDICATE WHEN THIS DOCUMENT SHALL BECOME EFFECTIVE, CHECK ONE OF THE FOLLOWING:

( ) This document shall become effective upon the date of my signature
( ) This document shall become effective upon the date of my disability and shall not otherwise be affected by my disability.

IF YOU HAVE INDICATED THAT THIS DOCUMENT SHALL BECOME EFFECTIVE ON THE DATE OF YOUR SIGNATURE, CHECK ONE OF THE FOLLOWING:

( ) This document shall not be affected by my subsequent disability.
( ) This document shall be revoked by my subsequent disability.

IF YOU HAVE INDICATED THAT THIS DOCUMENT SHALL BECOME EFFECTIVE UPON THE DATE OF YOUR SIGNATURE AND WANT TO LIMIT THE TERM OF THIS DOCUMENT, COMPLETE THE FOLLOWING:

This document shall only continue in effect for _____ ( ) years from the date of my signature.

NOTICE REGARDING REVOCATION OF THE POWERS GRANTED IN THIS DOCUMENT You may revoke one or more of the powers granted in this document. Unless otherwise provided in this document, you may revoke a specific power granted in this power of attorney by completing a special power of attorney that includes the specific power in this document that you want to revoke. Unless otherwise provided in this document, you may revoke all the powers granted in this power of attorney by completing a subsequent power of attorney

NOTICE TO THIRD PARTIES A third party who relies on the reasonable representations of an attorney-in-fact as to a matter relating to a power granted by a properly executed statutory power of attorney does not incur any liability to the principal or to the principal's heirs, assigns, or estate as a result of permitting the attorney-in-fact to exercise the authority granted by the power of attorney. A third party who fails to honor a properly executed statutory form power of attorney may be liable to the principal, the attorney-in-fact, the principal's heirs, assigns, or estate for a civil penalty, plus damages, costs, and fees associated with the failure to comply with the statutory form power of attorney. If the power of attorney is one which becomes effective upon the disability of the principal, the disability of the principal is established by an affidavit, as required by law

IN WITNESS WHEREOF, I have hereunto signed my name this _____ day of _____, 20_____.

_____
Signature of Principal

Notary Acknowledgement

Acknowledged before me at _____ on the following date:

_____.

_____
Signature of Officer or Notary

Arkansas Durable Power of Attorney

NOTICE: THE POWERS GRANTED BY THIS DOCUMENT ARE BROAD AND SWEEPING. THEY ARE EX-PLAINED IN THE UNIFORM STATUTORY FORM POWER OF ATTORNEY ACT. IF YOU HAVE ANY QUES-TIONS ABOUT THESE POWERS, OBTAIN COMPETENT LEGAL ADVICE. THIS DOCUMENT DOES NOT AUTHORIZE ANYONE TO MAKE MEDICAL AND OTHER HEALTH-CARE DECISIONS FOR YOU. YOU MAY REVOKE THIS POWER OF ATTORNEY IF YOU LATER WISH TO DO SO.

I _____ (name)
of _____ (address)
appoint _____ (name)
_____ (address)
as my agent (attorney-in-fact) to act for me in any lawful way with respect to the following initialed subjects:

TO GRANT ALL OF THE FOLLOWING POWERS, INITIAL THE LINE IN FRONT OF (N) AND IG-NORE THE LINES IN FRONT OF THE OTHER POWERS.

TO GRANT ONE OR MORE, BUT FEWER THAN ALL, OF THE FOLLOWING POWERS, INITIAL THE LINE IN FRONT OF EACH POWER YOU ARE GRANTING.

TO WITHHOLD A POWER, DO NOT INITIAL THE LINE IN FRONT OF IT. YOU MAY, BUT NEED NOT, CROSS OUT EACH POWER WITHHELD.

INITIAL

_____ (A) Real property transactions.
_____ (B) Tangible personal property transactions.
_____ (C) Stock and bond transactions.
_____ (D) Commodity and option transactions.
_____ (E) Banking and other financial institution transactions.
_____ (F) Business operating transactions.
_____ (G) Insurance and annuity transactions.
_____ (H) Estate, trust, and other beneficiary transactions.
_____ (I) Claims and litigation.
_____ (J) Personal and family maintenance.
_____ (K) Benefits from social security, medicare, medicaid, or other governmental programs, or military service.
_____ (L) Retirement plan transactions.
_____ (M) Tax matters.
_____ (N) ALL OF THE POWERS LISTED ABOVE. YOU NEED NOT INITIAL ANY OTHER LINES IF YOU INITIAL LINE (N).

SPECIAL INSTRUCTIONS: HERE YOU MAY GIVE SPECIAL INSTRUCTIONS LIMITING OR EXTENDING THE POWERS GRANTED TO YOUR AGENT.

UNLESS YOU DIRECT OTHERWISE ABOVE, THIS POWER OF ATTORNEY IS EFFECTIVE IMMEDIATELY AND WILL CONTINUE UNTIL IT IS REVOKED.

This power of attorney will continue to be effective even though I become disabled, incapacitated, or incompetent.

STRIKE THE PRECEDING SENTENCE IF YOU DO NOT WANT THIS POWER OF ATTORNEY TO CONTINUE IF YOU BECOME DISABLED, INCAPACITATED, OR INCOMPETENT.

I agree that any third party who receives a copy of this document may act under it. Revocation of the power of attorney is not effective as to a third party until the third party learns of the revocation. I agree to indemnify the third party for any claims that arise against the third party because of reliance on this power of attorney.

Signed this _____ day of _____ , 20_____

_____
Signature of Principal
_____
Social Security Number of Principal

Notary Acknowledgement

State of _____
County of _____

This document was acknowledged before me on _____ (Date) by
_____(Name of principal)

_____
(Signature of Notarial Officer)

(Seal, if any)

_____
(Title (and Rank))

My commission expires: _____

BY ACCEPTING OR ACTING UNDER THE APPOINTMENT, THE AGENT ASSUMES THE FIDUCIARY AND OTHER LEGAL RESPONSIBILITIES OF AN AGENT.

California Durable Power of Attorney

California Notice to Person Executing Durable Power of Attorney

A durable power of attorney is an important legal document. By signing the durable power of attorney, you are authorizing another person to act for you, the principal. Before you sign this durable power of attorney, you should know these important facts: Your agent (attorney-in-fact) has no duty to act unless you and your agent agree otherwise in writing. This document gives your agent the powers to manage, dispose of, sell, and convey your real and personal property, and to use your property as security if your agent borrows money on your behalf. This document does not give your agent the power to accept or receive any of your property, in trust or otherwise, as a gift, unless you specifically authorize the agent to accept or receive a gift. Your agent will have the right to receive reasonable payment for services provided under this durable power of attorney unless you provide otherwise in this power of attorney. The powers you give your agent will continue to exist for your entire lifetime, unless you state that the durable power of attorney will last for a shorter period of time or unless you otherwise terminate the durable power of attorney. The powers you give your agent in this durable power of attorney will continue to exist even if you can no longer make your own decisions respecting the management of your property. You can amend or change this durable power of attorney only by executing a new durable power of attorney or by executing an amendment through the same formalities as an original. You have the right to revoke or terminate this durable power of attorney at any time, so long as you are competent. This durable power of attorney must be dated and must be acknowledged before a notary public or signed by two witnesses. If it is signed by two witnesses, they must witness either (1) the signing of the power of attorney or (2) the principal's signing or acknowledgment of his or her signature. A durable power of attorney that may affect real property should be acknowledged before a notary public so that it may easily be recorded. You should read this durable power of attorney carefully. When effective, this durable power of attorney will give your agent the right to deal with property that you now have or might acquire in the future. The durable power of attorney is important to you. If you do not understand the durable power of attorney, or any provision of it, then you should obtain the assistance of an attorney or other qualified person.

NOTICE: THE POWERS GRANTED BY THIS DOCUMENT ARE BROAD AND SWEEPING. THEY ARE EXPLAINED IN THE CALIFORNIA PROBATE CODE, SECTIONS 4400-4465. IF YOU HAVE ANY QUESTIONS ABOUT THESE POWERS, OBTAIN COMPETENT LEGAL ADVICE. THIS DOCUMENT DOES NOT AUTHORIZE ANYONE TO MAKE MEDICAL AND OTHER HEALTH-CARE DECISIONS FOR YOU. YOU MAY REVOKE THIS POWER OF ATTORNEY IF YOU LATER WISH TO DO SO.

I _____ (name)
of _____ (address)
appoint _____ (name)
_____ (address)

as my agent (attorney-in-fact) to act for me in any lawful way with respect to the following initialed subjects:

TO GRANT ALL OF THE FOLLOWING POWERS, INITIAL THE LINE IN FRONT OF (N) AND IGNORE THE LINES IN FRONT OF THE OTHER POWERS.

TO GRANT ONE OR MORE, BUT FEWER THAN ALL, OF THE FOLLOWING POWERS, INITIAL THE LINE IN FRONT OF EACH POWER YOU ARE GRANTING.

TO WITHHOLD A POWER, DO NOT INITIAL THE LINE IN FRONT OF IT. YOU MAY, BUT NEED NOT, CROSS OUT EACH POWER WITHHELD.

INITIAL

_____ (A) Real property transactions.

_____ (B) Tangible personal property transactions.

_____ (C) Stock and bond transactions.

_____ (D) Commodity and option transactions.

_____ (E) Banking and other financial institution transactions.

_____ (F) Business operating transactions.

_____ (G) Insurance and annuity transactions.

_____ (H) Estate, trust, and other beneficiary transactions.

_____ (I) Claims and litigation.

_____ (J) Personal and family maintenance.

_____ (K) Benefits from social security, medicare, medicaid, or other governmental programs, or military service.

_____ (L) Retirement plan transactions.

_____ (M) Tax matters.

_____ (N) ALL OF THE POWERS LISTED ABOVE. YOU NEED NOT INITIAL ANY OTHER LINES IF YOU INITIAL LINE (N).

SPECIAL INSTRUCTIONS: HERE YOU MAY GIVE SPECIAL INSTRUCTIONS LIMITING OR EXTENDING THE POWERS GRANTED TO YOUR AGENT.

UNLESS YOU DIRECT OTHERWISE ABOVE, THIS POWER OF ATTORNEY IS EFFECTIVE IMMEDIATELY AND WILL CONTINUE UNTIL IT IS REVOKED.

This power of attorney will continue to be effective even though I become disabled, incapacitated, or incompetent.

STRIKE THE PRECEDING SENTENCE IF YOU DO NOT WANT THIS POWER OF ATTORNEY TO CONTINUE IF YOU BECOME DISABLED, INCAPACITATED, OR INCOMPETENT.

I agree that any third party who receives a copy of this document may act under it. Revocation of the power of attorney is not effective as to a third party until the third party learns of the revocation. I agree to indemnify the third party for any claims that arise against the third party because of reliance on this power of attorney.

Signed this _____ day of _____ , 20_____

_____
Signature of Principal

_____
Social Security Number of Principal

Notary Acknowledgement

State of California

County of _____

On this _____ day of _____ , 20_____ , before me, _____,
a notary public , personally appeared _____ , the principal,
personally known to me (or proved on the basis of satisfactory evidence) to be the person whose
name is subscribed to this instrument, and acknowledged that he/she executed it in his/her authorized
capacity, and that by his/her signature on this instrument the person executed this instrument.
Witness my hand and official Seal _____   Seal
                                              Signature of Notary Public

California Notice to Person Accepting the Appointment as Attorney-in-Fact

By acting or agreeing to act as the agent (attorney-in-fact) under this power of attorney you assume the fiduciary and other legal responsibilities of an agent. These responsibilities include: 1). The legal duty to act solely in the interest of the principal and to avoid conflicts of interest, and 2). The legal duty to keep the principal's property separate and distinct from any other property owned or controlled by you. You may not transfer the principal's property to yourself without full and adequate consideration or accept a gift of the principal's property unless this power of attorney specifically authorizes you to transfer property to yourself or accept a gift of the principal's property. If you transfer the principal's property to yourself without specific authorization in the power of attorney, you may be prosecuted for fraud and/or embezzlement. If the principal is 65 years of age or older at the time that the property is transferred to you without authority, you may also be prosecuted for elder abuse under Penal Code Section 368. In addition to criminal prosecution, you may also be sued in civil court. I have read the foregoing notice and I understand the legal and fiduciary duties that I assume by acting or agreeing to act as the agent (attorney-in-fact) under the terms of this power of attorney.

Date:

_____
(Signature of Agent)

_____
(Printed name of Agent)

Colorado Durable Power of Attorney

NOTICE: UNLESS YOU LIMIT THE POWER IN THIS DOCUMENT, THIS DOCUMENT GIVES YOUR AGENT THE POWER TO ACT FOR YOU, WITHOUT YOUR CONSENT, IN ANY WAY THAT YOU COULD ACT FOR YOURSELF. THE POWERS GRANTED BY THIS DOCUMENT ARE BROAD AND SWEEPING. THEY ARE EXPLAINED IN THE "UNIFORM STATUTORY FORM POWER OF ATTORNEY ACT", PART 13 OF ARTICLE 1 OF TITLE 15, COLORADO REVISED STATUTES, AND PART 6 OF ARTICLE 14 OF TITLE 15, COLORADO REVISED STATUTES. IF YOU HAVE ANY QUESTIONS ABOUT THESE POWERS, OBTAIN COMPETENT LEGAL ADVICE. THIS DOCUMENT DOES NOT AUTHORIZE ANYONE TO MAKE MEDICAL OR OTHER HEALTH-CARE DECISIONS FOR YOU. YOU MAY REVOKE THIS POWER OF ATTORNEY IF YOU LATER WISH TO DO SO.

THE PURPOSE OF THIS POWER OF ATTORNEY IS TO GIVE THE PERSON YOU DESIGNATE (YOUR "AGENT") BROAD POWERS TO HANDLE YOUR PROPERTY AND AFFAIRS, WHICH MAY INCLUDE POWERS TO PLEDGE, SELL, OR OTHERWISE DISPOSE OF ANY REAL OR PERSONAL PROPERTY WITHOUT ADVANCE NOTICE TO YOU OR APPROVAL BY YOU. THIS FORM DOES NOT IMPOSE A DUTY ON YOUR AGENT TO EXERCISE GRANTED POWERS; BUT WHEN POWERS ARE EXERCISED, YOUR AGENT MUST USE DUE CARE TO ACT FOR YOUR BENEFIT AND IN ACCORDANCE WITH THE PROVISIONS OF THIS FORM AND MUST KEEP A RECORD OF RECEIPTS, DISBURSEMENTS, AND SIGNIFICANT ACTIONS TAKEN AS AGENT. YOU MAY NAME SUCCESSOR AGENTS UNDER THIS FORM BUT NOT CO-AGENTS. UNTIL YOU REVOKE THIS POWER OF ATTORNEY OR A COURT ACTING ON YOUR BEHALF TERMINATES IT, YOUR AGENT MAY EXERCISE THE POWERS GIVEN HERE THROUGHOUT YOUR LIFETIME, EVEN AFTER YOU MAY BECOME DISABLED, UNLESS YOU EXPRESSLY LIMIT THE DURATION OF THIS POWER IN THE MANNER PROVIDED BELOW.

YOU MAY HAVE OTHER RIGHTS OR POWERS UNDER COLORADO LAW NOT SPECIFIED IN THIS FORM.

I,_____, (name)
_____(address),
appoint_____, (name)
_____(address),
as my agent (attorney-in-fact) to act for me in any lawful way with respect to the following initialed subjects:

TO GRANT ONE OR MORE OF THE FOLLOWING POWERS, INITIAL THE LINE IN FRONT OF EACH POWER YOU ARE GRANTING. TO WITHHOLD A POWER, DO NOT INITIAL THE LINE IN FRONT OF IT. YOU MAY, BUT NEED NOT, CROSS OUT EACH POWER WITHHELD.
INITIAL

_____ (A) Real property transactions (when properly recorded).
_____ (B) Tangible personal property transactions.
_____ (C) Stock and bond transactions.
_____ (D) Commodity and option transactions.
_____ (E) Banking and other financial institution transactions.
_____ (F) Business operating transactions.
_____ (G) Insurance and annuity transactions.
_____ (H) Estate, trust, and other beneficiary transactions.

_____   (I) Claims and litigation.
_____   (J) Personal and family maintenance.
_____   (K) Benefits from social security, medicare, medicaid,
                or other governmental programs or military service.
_____   (L) Retirement plan transactions.
_____   (M) Tax matters.

UNLESS YOU DIRECT OTHERWISE, THIS POWER OF ATTORNEY IS EFFECTIVE IMMEDIATELY AND WILL CONTINUE UNTIL IT IS REVOKED OR TERMINATED AS SPECIFIED BELOW. STRIKE THROUGH AND WRITE YOUR INITIALS TO THE LEFT OF THE FOLLOWING SENTENCE IF YOU DO NOT WANT THIS POWER OF ATTORNEY TO CONTINUE IF YOU BECOME DISABLED, INCAPACITATED, OR INCOMPETENT.

1. (   ) This power of attorney will continue to be effective even though I become disabled, incapacitated, or incompetent.

YOU MAY INCLUDE ADDITIONS TO AND LIMITATIONS ON THE AGENT'S POWERS IN THIS POWER OF ATTORNEY IF THEY ARE SPECIFICALLY DESCRIBED BELOW.

2. The powers granted above shall not include the following powers or shall be modified or limited in the following manner (here you may include any specific limitations you deem appropriate, such as a prohibition of or conditions on the sale of particular stock or real estate or special rules regarding borrowing by the agent):

3. In addition to the powers granted above, I grant my agent the following powers (here you may add any other delegable powers, such as the power to make gifts, exercise powers of appointment, name or change beneficiaries or joint tenants, or revoke or amend any trust specifically referred to below):

4. SPECIAL INSTRUCTIONS. ON THE FOLLOWING LINES YOU MAY GIVE SPECIAL INSTRUCTIONS TO YOUR AGENT:

YOUR AGENT WILL BE ENTITLED TO REIMBURSEMENT FOR ALL REASONABLE EXPENSES INCURRED IN ACTING UNDER THIS POWER OF ATTORNEY. STRIKE THROUGH AND INITIAL THE NEXT SENTENCE IF YOU DO NOT WANT YOUR AGENT TO ALSO BE ENTITLED TO REASONABLE COMPENSATION FOR SERVICES AS AGENT.

5. (   ) My agent is entitled to reasonable compensation for services rendered as agent under this power of attorney.

THIS POWER OF ATTORNEY MAY BE AMENDED IN ANY MANNER OR REVOKED BY YOU AT ANY TIME. ABSENT AMENDMENT OR REVOCATION, THE AUTHORITY GRANTED IN THIS POWER OF ATTORNEY IS EFFECTIVE WHEN THIS POWER OF ATTORNEY IS SIGNED AND CONTINUES IN EFFECT UNTIL YOUR DEATH, UNLESS YOU MAKE A LIMITATION ON DURATION BY COMPLETING THE FOLLOWING:

6. This power of attorney terminates on _____. (Insert a future date or event, such as court determination of your disability, when you want this power to terminate prior to your death).

BY RETAINING THE FOLLOWING PARAGRAPH, YOU MAY, BUT ARE NOT REQUIRED TO, NAME YOUR AGENT AS GUARDIAN OF YOUR PERSON OR CONSERVATOR OF YOUR PROPERTY, OR BOTH, IF A COURT PROCEEDING IS BEGUN TO APPOINT A GUARDIAN OR CONSERVATOR, OR BOTH, FOR YOU. THE COURT WILL APPOINT YOUR AGENT AS GUARDIAN OR CONSERVATOR, OR BOTH, IF THE COURT FINDS THAT SUCH APPOINTMENT WILL SERVE YOUR BEST INTERESTS AND WELFARE. STRIKE THROUGH AND INITIAL PARAGRAPH 7 IF YOU DO NOT WANT YOUR AGENT TO ACT AS GUARDIAN OR CONSERVATOR, OR BOTH.

7. (   ) If a guardian of my person or a conservator for my property, or both, are to be appointed, I nominate the agent acting under this power of attorney as such guardian or conservator, or both, to serve without bond or security.

IF YOU WISH TO NAME SUCCESSOR AGENTS, INSERT THE NAME AND ADDRESS OF ANY SUCCESSOR AGENT IN THE FOLLOWING PARAGRAPH:

8. If any agent named by me shall die, become incapacitated, resign, or refuse to accept the office of agent, I name the following each to act alone and successively, in the order named, as successor to such agent:

For purposes of this paragraph 8, a person is considered to be incapacitated if and while the person is a minor or a person adjudicated incapacitated or if the person is unable to give prompt and intelligent consideration to business matters, as certified by a licensed physician.

I agree that any third party who receives a copy of this document may act under it. Revocation of the power of attorney is not effective as to a third party until the third party learns of the revocation. I agree to indemnify the third party for any claims that arise against the third party because of reliance on this power of attorney.

Signed on_____, 20____

IF THERE IS ANYTHING ABOUT THIS FORM THAT YOU DO NOT UNDERSTAND, IT MAY BE IN YOUR BEST INTEREST TO CONSULT A COLORADO LAWYER RATHER THAN SIGN THIS FORM.

_____
(Your Signature)

_____
(Your Social Security Number)

YOU MAY, BUT ARE NOT REQUIRED TO, REQUEST YOUR AGENT AND SUCCESSOR AGENTS TO PROVIDE SPECIMEN SIGNATURES BELOW. IF YOU INCLUDE SPECIMEN SIGNATURES IN THIS POWER OF ATTORNEY, YOU MUST COMPLETE THE CERTIFICATION OPPOSITE THE SIGNATURES OF THE AGENTS.

NOTICE TO AGENTS: BY EXERCISING POWERS UNDER THIS DOCUMENT, THE AGENT ASSUMES THE FIDUCIARY AND OTHER LEGAL RESPONSIBILITIES OF AN AGENT UNDER COLORADO LAW.

Specimen Signatures of Agent

I certify that the signatures of my agent (and successor) are correct.

_____
Signature of Principal

_____
Signature of Agent

_____
Signature of Successor Agent

Notary Acknowledgement

STATE OF COLORADO
County of _____)

This document was acknowledged before me on _____ (date) by _____ (name of principal). who certifies the correctness of the signature(s) of the agent(s).

My commission expires: _____   [Seal]

_____
Signature of Notary Public

Connecticut Durable Power of Attorney

Notice: The powers granted by this document are broad and sweeping. They are defined in Connecticut Statutory Short Form Power of Attorney Act, sections 1-42 to 1-56, inclusive, of the general statutes, which expressly permits the use of any other or different form of power of attorney desired by the parties concerned. The grantor of any power of attorney or the attorney-in-fact may make application to a court of probate for an accounting as provided in subsection (b) of section 45a-175.

Know All Men by These Presents, which are intended to constitute a GENERAL POWER OF ATTORNEY pursuant to Connecticut Statutory Short Form Power of Attorney Act:

That I_____ (name)
_____(address)
do hereby appoint_____ (name)
_____(address)
as my attorney-in-fact TO ACT _____

If more than one agent is designated and the principal wishes each agent alone to be able to exercise the power conferred, insert in this blank the word `severally'. Failure to make any insertion or the insertion of the word `jointly' shall require the agents to act jointly.

First: In my name, place and stead in any way which I myself could do, if I were personally present, with respect to the following matters as each of them is defined in the Connecticut Statutory Short Form Power of Attorney Act to the extent that I am permitted by law to act through an agent:

(Strike out and initial in the opposite box any one or more of the subdivisions as to which the principal does NOT desire to give the agent authority. Such elimination of any one or more of subdivisions (A) to (L), inclusive, shall automatically constitute an elimination also of subdivision (M). To strike out any subdivision the principal must draw a line through the text of that subdivision AND write his initials in the box opposite.)

(A)   real estate transactions;   (   )
(B)   chattel and goods transactions; (   )
(C)   bond, share and commodity transactions;   (   )
(D)   banking transactions;   (   )
(E)   business operating transactions;   (   )
(F)   insurance transactions; (   )
(G)   estate transactions;   (   )
(H)   claims and litigation;   (   )
(I)   personal relationships and affairs;   (   )
(J)   benefits from military service; (   )
(K)   records, reports and statements;   (   )
(L)   health care decisions;   (   )
(M)   all other matters;   (   )

(Special provisions and limitations may be included in the statutory short form power of attorney only if they conform to the requirements of the Connecticut Statutory Short Form Power of Attorney Act.)

Second: With full and unqualified authority to delegate any or all of the foregoing powers to any person or persons whom my attorney(s)-in-fact shall select:

Third: Hereby ratifying and confirming all that said attorney(s) or substitute(s) do or cause to be done.

Signature of Principal

In Witness Whereof I have hereunto signed my name and affixed my seal this_____day of_____, 20_____.

_____
(Signature of Principal)

Witness Attestation

On the date written above, the principal declared to us that this instrument was his/her durable power of attorney, and requested us to act as witnesses to it. He/she signed it in our presence, all of us being present at the same time. We now sign this instrument as witnesses.

_____
(Signature of First Witness)
_____
(Signature of Second Witness)

Acknowledgement

State of Connecticut
County of_____
The foregoing instrument was acknowledged before me this_____day of_____, 20_____.

_____
Official Signature   (Seal)
Serial Number if any_____   Title or Rank _____

Washington DC Durable Power of Attorney

NOTICE: THE POWERS GRANTED BY THIS DOCUMENT ARE BROAD AND SWEEPING. THEY ARE EXPLAINED IN THE UNIFORM STATUTORY FORM POWER OF ATTORNEY ACT OF 1998. IF YOU HAVE ANY QUESTIONS ABOUT THESE POWERS, OBTAIN COMPETENT LEGAL ADVICE. THIS DOCUMENT DOES NOT AUTHORIZE ANYONE TO MAKE MEDICAL AND OTHER HEALTH-CARE DECISIONS FOR YOU. YOU MAY REVOKE THIS POWER OF ATTORNEY IF YOU LATER WISH TO DO SO.

I _____ (name)

_____ (address)

do hereby appoint _____ (name)

_____ (address)

as my agent (attorney-in-fact) to act for me in any lawful way with respect to the following initialed subjects:

TO GRANT ALL OF THE FOLLOWING POWERS, INITIAL THE LINE IN FRONT OF (N) AND IGNORE THE LINES IN FRONT OF THE OTHER POWERS. YOU NEED NOT INITIAL ANY OTHER LINES IF YOU INITIAL LINE (N).

TO GRANT ONE OR MORE, BUT FEWER THAN ALL, OF THE FOLLOWING POWERS, INITIAL THE LINE IN FRONT OF EACH POWER YOU ARE GRANTING.

TO WITHHOLD A POWER, DO NOT INITIAL THE LINE IN FRONT OF IT. YOU MAY, BUT NEED NOT, CROSS OUT EACH POWER WITHHELD.

INITIAL

_____ (A) Real property transactions, except transactions subject to D.C. Official Code § 42-101.

_____ (B) Tangible personal property transactions.

_____ (C) Stock and bond transactions.

_____ (D) Commodity and option transactions.

_____ (E) Banking and other financial institution transactions.

_____ (F) Business operating transactions.

_____ (G) Insurance and annuity transactions.

_____ (H) Estate, trust, and other beneficiary transactions.

_____ (I) Claims and litigation.

_____ (J) Personal and family maintenance.

_____ (K) Benefits from social security, medicare, medicaid, or other governmental programs, or military service.

_____ (L) Retirement plan transactions.

_____ (M) Tax matters.

_____ (N) ALL OF THE POWERS LISTED ABOVE.

SPECIAL INSTRUCTIONS: ON THE FOLLOWING LINES YOU MAY GIVE SPECIAL INSTRUCTIONS LIMITING OR EXTENDING THE POWERS GRANTED TO YOUR AGENT:

UNLESS YOU DIRECT OTHERWISE ABOVE, THIS POWER OF ATTORNEY IS EFFECTIVE IMMEDIATELY AND WILL CONTINUE UNTIL IT IS REVOKED.

This power of attorney will continue to be effective even though I become disabled, incapacitated, or incompetent.

STRIKE THE PRECEDING SENTENCE IF YOU DO NOT WANT THIS POWER OF ATTORNEY TO CONTINUE IF YOU BECOME DISABLED, INCAPACITATED, OR INCOMPETENT.

I agree that any third party who receives a copy of this document may act under it. Revocation of the power of attorney is not effective as to a third party until the third party learns of the revocation. I agree to indemnify the third party for any claims that arise against the third party because of reliance on this power of attorney.

Signed this _____ day of _____, 20 _____

_____
(Your Signature)

_____
(Your Social Security Number)

Notary Acknowledgement

District of Columbia

This document was acknowledged before me on _____ (Date) by
_____ (name of principal)

_____
(Signature of Notary Public)

(Seal)

My commission expires: _____

BY ACCEPTING OR ACTING UNDER THE APPOINTMENT, THE AGENT ASSUMES THE FIDUCIARY AND OTHER LEGAL RESPONSIBILITIES OF AN AGENT.

Georgia Durable Power of Attorney

County of _____
State of Georgia

I, _____, (hereinafter 'Principal'), a resident of _____ County, Georgia, do hereby constitute and appoint _____ my true and lawful attorney-in-fact (hereinafter 'Agent') for me and give such person the power(s) specified below to act in my name, place, and stead in any way which I, myself, could do if I were personally present with respect to the following matters:

(Directions: To give the Agent the powers described in paragraphs 1 through 13, place your initials on the blank line at the end of each paragraph. If you DO NOT want to give a power to the Agent, strike through the paragraph or a line within the paragraph and place your initials beside the stricken paragraph or stricken line. The powers described in any paragraph not initialed or which has been struck through will not be conveyed to the Agent. Both the Principal and the Agent must sign their full names at the end of the last paragraph.)

1. Bank and Credit Union Transactions: To make, receive, sign, endorse, execute, acknowledge, deliver, and possess checks, drafts, bills of exchange, letters of credit, notes, stock certificates, withdrawal receipts and deposit instruments relating to accounts or deposits in, or certificates of deposit of banks, savings and loans, credit unions, or other institutions or associations._____ (initial or strike through paragraph)

2. Payment Transactions: To pay all sums of money, at any time or times, that may hereafter be owing by me upon any account, bill or exchange, check, draft, purchase, contract, note, or trade acceptance made, executed, endorsed, accepted, and delivered by me or for me in my name, by my Agent._____ (initial or strike through paragraph)

Note: If you initial paragraph 3 or paragraph 4 which follow, a notarized signature will be required on behalf of the Principal.

3. Real Property Transactions: To lease, sell, mortgage, purchase, exchange, and acquire, and to agree, bargain, and contract for the lease, sale, purchase, exchange, and acquisition of, and to accept, take, receive, and possess any interest in real property whatsoever, on such terms and conditions, and under such covenants, as my Agent shall deem proper; and to maintain, repair, tear down, alter, rebuild, improve, manage, insure, move, rent, lease, sell, convey, subject to liens, mortgages, and security deeds, and in any way or manner deal with all or any part of any interest in real property whatsoever, including specifically, but without limitation, real property lying and being situate in the State of Georgia, under such terms and conditions, and under such covenants, as my Agent shall deem proper and may for all deferred payments accept purchase money notes payable to me and secured by mortgages or deeds to secure debt, and may from time to time collect and cancel any of said notes, mortgages, security interests, or deeds to secure debt. _____ (initial or strike through paragraph)

4. Personal Property Transactions: To lease, sell, mortgage, purchase, exchange, and acquire, and to agree, bargain, and contract for the lease, sale, purchase, exchange, and acquisition of, and to accept, take, receive, and possess any personal property whatsoever, tangible or intangible, or interest thereto, on such terms and conditions, and under such covenants, as my Agent shall deem proper; and to maintain, repair, improve, manage, insure, rent, lease, sell, convey, subject to liens or mortgages, or to take any other security interests in said property which are recognized under the Uniform Commercial Code as adopted at that time under the laws of Georgia or any applicable state, or otherwise hypothecate, and in any way or manner deal with all or any part of any real or personal property whatsoever, tangible or intangible, or any interest therein, that I own at the time of execution or may thereafter acquire, under such terms and conditions, and under such covenants, as my Agent shall deem proper. _____ (initial or strike through paragraph)

5. Stock and Bond Transactions: To purchase, sell, exchange, surrender, assign, redeem, vote at any meeting, or otherwise transfer any and all shares of stock, bonds, or other securities in any business, association, corporation, partnership, or other legal entity, whether private or public, now or hereafter belonging to me. _____ (initial or strike through paragraph)

6. Safe Deposits: To have free access at any time or times to any safe-deposit box or vault to which I might have access. _____ (initial or strike through paragraph)

7. Borrowing: To borrow from time to time such sums of money as my Agent may deem proper and execute promissory notes, security deeds or agreements, financing statements, or other security instruments in such form as the lender may request and renew said notes and security instruments from time to time in whole or in part. _____ (initial or strike through paragraph)

8. Business Operating Transactions: To conduct, engage in, and otherwise transact the affairs of any and all lawful business ventures of whatever nature or kind that I may now or hereafter be involved in. _____ (initial or strike through paragraph)

9. Insurance Transactions: To exercise or perform any act, power, duty, right, or obligation, in regard to any contract of life, accident, health, disability, liability, or other type of insurance or any combination of insurance; and to procure new or additional contracts of insurance for me and to designate the beneficiary of same; provided, however, that my Agent cannot designate himself or herself as beneficiary of any such insurance contracts. _____ (initial or strike through paragraph)

10. Disputes and Proceedings: To commence, prosecute, discontinue, or defend all actions or other legal proceedings touching my property, real or personal, or any part thereof, or touching any matter in which I or my property, real or personal, may be in any way concerned. To defend, settle, adjust, make allowances, compound, submit to arbitration, and compromise all accounts, reckonings, claims, and demands whatsoever that now are, or hereafter shall be, pending between me and any person, firm, corporation, or other legal entity, in such manner and in all respects as my Agent shall deem proper. _____ (initial or strike through paragraph)

11. Hiring Representatives: To hire accountants, attorneys at law, consultants, clerks, physicians, nurses, agents, servants, workmen, and others and to remove them, and to appoint others in their place, and to pay and allow the persons so employed such salaries, wages, or other remunerations, as my Agent shall deem proper. _____ **(initial or strike through paragraph)**

12. Tax, Social Security, and Unemployment: To prepare, to make elections, to execute and to file all tax, social security, unemployment insurance, and informational returns required by the laws of the United States, or of any state or subdivision thereof, or of any foreign government; to prepare, to execute, and to file all other papers and instruments which the Agent shall think to be desirable or necessary for safeguarding of me against excess or illegal taxation or against penalties imposed for claimed violation of any law or other governmental regulation; and to pay, to compromise, or to contest or to apply for refunds in connection with any taxes or assessments for which I am or may be liable. _____ **(initial or strike through paragraph)**

13. Broad Powers: Without, in any way, limiting the foregoing, generally to do, execute, and perform any other act, deed, matter, or thing whatsoever, that should be done, executed, or performed, including, but not limited to, powers conferred by Code Section 53-12-232 of the Official Code of Georgia Annotated, or that in the opinion of my Agent, should be done, executed, or performed, for my benefit or the benefit of my property, real or personal, and in my name of every nature and kind whatsoever, as fully and effectually as I could do if personally present. _____ **(initial or strike through paragraph)**

14. Effective Date: This document will become effective upon the date of the Principal's signature unless the Principal indicates that it should become effective at a later date by completing the following, which is optional.

The powers conveyed in this document shall not become effective until the following time or upon the occurrence of the following event or contingency:_____
_____.

Note: The Principal may choose to designate one or more persons to determine conclusively that the above-specified event or contingency has occurred. Such person or persons must make a written declaration under penalty of false swearing that such event or contingency has occurred in order to make this document effective. Completion of this provision is optional.

The following person or persons are designated to determine conclusively that the above-specified event or contingency has occurred:

_____
_____

_____
Signature of Principal

_____
Signature of Agent

It is my desire and intention that this power of attorney shall not be affected by my subsequent disability, incapacity, or mental incompetence. However, I understand that it shall be revoked and the Agent's power canceled in the event a guardian is appointed for my property. As long as no such guardian is appointed, any and all acts done by the Agent pursuant to the powers conveyed herein during any period of my disability, incapacity, or mental incompetence shall have the same force and effect as if I were not disabled, incapacitated, or mentally incompetent. I may, at any time, revoke this power of attorney, and it shall be canceled by my death. Otherwise, unless a guardian is appointed for my property, this power of attorney shall be deemed to be in full force and effect as to all persons, institutions, and organizations which shall act in reliance thereon prior to the receipt of written revocation thereof signed by me and prior to my death.

I do hereby ratify and confirm all acts whatsoever which my Agent shall do, or cause to be done, in or about the premises, by virtue of this power of attorney.

All parties dealing in good faith with my Agent may fully rely upon the power of and authority of my Agent to act for me on my behalf and in my name, and may accept and rely on agreements and other instruments entered into or executed by the agent pursuant to this power of attorney.

This instrument shall not be effective as a grant of powers to my Agent until my Agent has executed the Acceptance of Appointment appearing at the end of this instrument. This instrument shall remain effective until revocation by me or my death, whichever occurs first.

Compensation of Agent. **(Directions: Initial the line following your choice.)**
1. My Agent shall receive no compensation for services rendered. _____
2. My Agent shall receive reasonable compensation for services rendered. _____
3. My Agent shall receive $_____ for services rendered. _____

IN WITNESS WHEREOF, I have hereunto set my hand and seal on this _____ day of _____, 20_____.

_____
Signature of Principal

Witness Attestation

_____
Signature of Witness

_____
Address

_____
Signature of Witness

_____
Address

Note: A notarized signature of the principal is not required unless you have initialed paragraph 3 or 4 regarding property transactions.

I, _____, a Notary Public, do hereby certify that
_____ personally appeared before me
this date and acknowledged the due execution of the foregoing Power of Attorney.

_____

Signature of Notary Public

State of Georgia   County of _____

Acceptance Of Appointment by Agent

I, _____ (print name), have read
the foregoing Power of Attorney and am the person identified therein as Agent for
_____ (name of grantor of power of
attorney), the Principal named therein. I hereby acknowledge the following:

I owe a duty of loyalty and good faith to the Principal, and must use the powers granted to me only for the benefit of the Principal. I must keep the Principal´s funds and other assets separate and apart from my funds and other assets and titled in the name of the Principal. I must not transfer title to any of the Principal´s funds or other assets into my name alone. My name must not be added to the title of any funds or other assets of the Principal, unless I am specifically designated as Agent for the Principal in the title. I must protect, conserve, and exercise prudence and caution in my dealings with the Principal´s funds and other assets. I must keep a full and accurate record of my acts, receipts, and disbursements on behalf of the Principal, and be ready to account to the Principal for such acts, receipts, and disbursements at all times. I must provide an annual accounting to the Principal of my acts, receipts, and disbursements, and must furnish an accounting of such acts, receipts, and disbursements to the personal representative of the Principal´s estate within 90 days after the date of death of the Principal. I have read the Compensation of Agent paragraph in the Power of Attorney and agree to abide by it. I acknowledge my authority to act on behalf of the Principal ceases at the death of the Principal. I hereby accept the foregoing appointment as Agent for the Principal with full knowledge of the responsibilities imposed on me, and I will faithfully carry out my duties to the best of my ability.

Dated:_____, 20____.

(Signature of Agent)_____
(Address)_____

Note: A notarized signature of the agent is not required unless the Principal initialed paragraph 3 or paragraph 4 regarding property transactions.

I, _____, a Notary Public, do hereby certify that
_____ personally appeared before me this
date and acknowledge the due execution of the foregoing Acceptance of Appointment.

_____

Signature of Notary Public

Illinois Durable Power of Attorney

(NOTICE: THE PURPOSE OF THIS POWER OF ATTORNEY IS TO GIVE THE PERSON YOU DESIGNATE (YOUR "AGENT") BROAD POWERS TO HANDLE YOUR PROPERTY, WHICH MAY INCLUDE POWERS TO PLEDGE, SELL OR OTHERWISE DISPOSE OF ANY REAL OR PERSONAL PROPERTY WITHOUT ADVANCE NOTICE TO YOU OR APPROVAL BY YOU. THIS FORM DOES NOT IMPOSE A DUTY ON YOUR AGENT TO EXERCISE GRANTED POWERS; BUT WHEN POWERS ARE EXERCISED, YOUR AGENT WILL HAVE TO USE DUE CARE TO ACT FOR YOUR BENEFIT AND IN ACCORDANCE WITH THIS FORM AND KEEP A RECORD OF RECEIPTS, DISBURSEMENTS AND SIGNIFICANT ACTIONS TAKEN AS AGENT. A COURT CAN TAKE AWAY THE POWERS OF YOUR AGENT IF IT FINDS THE AGENT IS NOT ACTING PROPERLY. YOU MAY NAME SUCCESSOR AGENTS UNDER THIS FORM BUT NOT CO-AGENTS. UNLESS YOU EXPRESSLY LIMIT THE DURATION OF THIS POWER IN THE MANNER PROVIDED BELOW, UNTIL YOU REVOKE THIS POWER OR A COURT ACTING ON YOUR BEHALF TERMINATES IT, YOUR AGENT MAY EXERCISE THE POWERS GIVEN HERE THROUGHOUT YOUR LIFETIME, EVEN AFTER YOU BECOME DISABLED. THE POWERS YOU GIVE YOUR AGENT ARE EXPLAINED MORE FULLY IN SECTION 3-4 OF THE ILLINOIS "STATUTORY SHORT FORM POWER OF ATTORNEY FOR PROPERTY LAW" OF WHICH THIS FORM IS A PART (SEE THE BACK OF THIS FORM). THAT LAW EXPRESSLY PERMITS THE USE OF ANY DIFFERENT FORM OF POWER OF ATTORNEY YOU MAY DESIRE. IF THERE IS ANYTHING ABOUT THIS FORM THAT YOU DO NOT UNDERSTAND, YOU SHOULD ASK A LAWYER TO EXPLAIN IT TO YOU.)

POWER OF ATTORNEY made this_____day of_____, 20_____

1. I,_____ (name)

_____(address) do

hereby appoint_____ (name)

_____(address) as

my attorney-in-fact (my "agent") to act for me and in my name (in any way I could act in person) with respect to the following powers, as defined in Section 3-4 of the "Statutory Short Form Power of Attorney for Property Law" (including all amendments), but subject to any limitations on or additions to the specified powers inserted in paragraph 2 or 3 below:

(YOU MUST STRIKE OUT ANY ONE OR MORE OF THE FOLLOWING CATEGORIES OF POWERS YOU DO NOT WANT YOUR AGENT TO HAVE. FAILURE TO STRIKE THE TITLE OF ANY CATEGORY WILL CAUSE THE POWERS DESCRIBED IN THAT CATEGORY TO BE GRANTED TO THE AGENT. TO STRIKE OUT A CATEGORY YOU MUST DRAW A LINE THROUGH THE TITLE OF THAT CATEGORY.)

(a) Real estate transactions.
(b) Financial institution transactions.
(c) Stock and bond transactions.
(d) Tangible personal property transactions.
(e) Safe deposit box transactions.
(f) Insurance and annuity transactions.
(g) Retirement plan transactions.
(h) Social Security, employment and military service benefits.

(i) Tax matters.

(j) Claims and litigation.

(k) Commodity and option transactions.

(l) Business operations.

(m) Borrowing transactions.

(n) Estate transactions.

(o) All other property powers and transactions.

(LIMITATIONS ON AND ADDITIONS TO THE AGENT'S POWERS MAY BE INCLUDED IN THIS POWER OF ATTORNEY IF THEY ARE SPECIFICALLY DESCRIBED BELOW.)

2. The powers granted above shall not include the following powers or shall be modified or limited in the following particulars **(here you may include any specific limitations you deem appropriate, such as a prohibition or conditions on the sale of particular stock or real estate or special rules on borrowing by the agent):**

3. In addition to the powers granted above, I grant my agent the following powers **(here you may add any other delegable powers including, without limitation, power to make gifts, exercise powers of appointment, name or change beneficiaries or joint tenants or revoke or amend any trust specifically referred to below):**

(YOUR AGENT WILL HAVE AUTHORITY TO EMPLOY OTHER PERSONS AS NECESSARY TO ENABLE THE AGENT TO PROPERLY EXERCISE THE POWERS GRANTED IN THIS FORM, BUT YOUR AGENT WILL HAVE TO MAKE ALL DISCRETIONARY DECISIONS. IF YOU WANT TO GIVE YOUR AGENT THE RIGHT TO DELEGATE DISCRETIONARY DECISION-MAKING POWERS TO OTHERS, YOU SHOULD KEEP THE NEXT SENTENCE, OTHERWISE IT SHOULD BE STRUCK OUT.)

4. My agent shall have the right by written instrument to delegate any or all of the foregoing powers involving discretionary decision-making to any person or persons whom my agent may select, but such delegation may be amended or revoked by any agent (including any successor) named by me who is acting under this power of attorney at the time of reference.

(YOUR AGENT WILL BE ENTITLED TO REIMBURSEMENT FOR ALL REASONABLE EXPENSES INCURRED IN ACTING UNDER THIS POWER OF ATTORNEY. STRIKE OUT THE NEXT SENTENCE IF YOU DO NOT WANT YOUR AGENT TO ALSO BE ENTITLED TO REASONABLE COMPENSATION FOR SERVICES AS AGENT.)

5. My agent shall be entitled to reasonable compensation for services rendered as agent under this power of attorney.

(THIS POWER OF ATTORNEY MAY BE AMENDED OR REVOKED BY YOU AT ANY TIME AND IN

ANY MANNER. ABSENT AMENDMENT OR REVOCATION, THE AUTHORITY GRANTED IN THIS POWER OF ATTORNEY WILL BECOME EFFECTIVE AT THE TIME THIS POWER IS SIGNED AND WILL CONTINUE UNTIL YOUR DEATH UNLESS A LIMITATION ON THE BEGINNING DATE OR DURATION IS MADE BY INITIALING AND COMPLETING EITHER (OR BOTH) OF THE FOLLOWING:)

6. (   ) This power of attorney shall become effective on_____
(insert a future date or event during your lifetime, such as court determination of your disability, when you want this power to first take effect).

7. (   ) This power of attorney shall terminate on_____.
(insert a future date or event, such as court determination of your disability, when you want this power to terminate prior to your death)

(IF YOU WISH TO NAME SUCCESSOR AGENTS, INSERT THE NAME(S) AND ADDRESS(ES) OF SUCH SUCCESSOR(S) IN THE FOLLOWING PARAGRAPH.)

8. If any agent named by me shall die, become incompetent, resign or refuse to accept the office of agent, I name the following (each to act alone and successively, in the order named) as successor(s) to such agent:

_____

_____

For purposes of this paragraph 8, a person shall be considered to be incompetent if and while the person is a minor or an adjudicated incompetent or disabled person or the person is unable to give prompt and intelligent consideration to business matters, as certified by a licensed physician.

(IF YOU WISH TO NAME YOUR AGENT AS GUARDIAN OF YOUR ESTATE, IN THE EVENT A COURT DECIDES THAT ONE SHOULD BE APPOINTED, YOU MAY, BUT ARE NOT REQUIRED TO, DO SO BY RETAINING THE FOLLOWING PARAGRAPH. THE COURT WILL APPOINT YOUR AGENT IF THE COURT FINDS THAT SUCH APPOINTMENT WILL SERVE YOUR BEST INTERESTS AND WELFARE. STRIKE OUT PARAGRAPH 9 IF YOU DO NOT WANT YOUR AGENT TO ACT AS GUARDIAN.)

9. If a guardian of my estate (my property) is to be appointed, I nominate the agent acting under this power of attorney as such guardian, to serve without bond or security.

10. I am fully informed as to all the contents of this form and understand the full import of this grant of powers to my agent.

_____
Signature of Principal

(YOU MAY, BUT ARE NOT REQUIRED TO, REQUEST YOUR AGENT AND SUCCESSOR AGENTS TO PROVIDE SPECIMEN SIGNATURES BELOW. IF YOU INCLUDE SPECIMEN SIGNATURES IN THIS POWER OF ATTORNEY, YOU MUST COMPLETE THE CERTIFICATION OPPOSITE THE SIGNATURES OF THE AGENTS.)

Specimen Signatures of Agent (and Successors)

I certify that the signatures of my agent (and successors) are correct.

_____
Signature of Principal

_____
Signature of agent

_____
Signature of successor agent

(THIS POWER OF ATTORNEY WILL NOT BE EFFECTIVE UNLESS IT IS NOTARIZED AND SIGNED BY AT LEAST ONE ADDITIONAL WITNESS, USING THE FORM BELOW.)

Notary Acknowledgement

State of _____)SS.

County of_____)

The undersigned, a notary public in and for the above county and state, certifies that _____, known to me to be the same person whose name is subscribed as principal to the foregoing power of attorney, appeared before me and the additional witness in person and acknowledged signing and delivering the instrument as the free and voluntary act of the principal, for the uses and purposes therein set forth (, and certified to the correctness of the signature(s) of the agent(s)).

Dated:_____   (SEAL)

_____
Signature of Notary Public

My commission expires _____

Witness Attestation

The undersigned witness certifies that_____, known to me to be the same person whose name is subscribed as principal to the foregoing power of attorney, appeared before me and the notary public and acknowledged signing and delivering the instrument as the free and voluntary act of the principal, for the uses and purposes therein set forth. I believe him or her to be of sound mind and memory.

Dated:_____

_____
Signature of Witness

(THE NAME AND ADDRESS OF THE PERSON PREPARING THIS FORM SHOULD BE INSERTED IF THE AGENT WILL HAVE POWER TO CONVEY ANY INTEREST IN REAL ESTATE.)

This document was prepared by:_____(name)

_____(address)

Montana Durable Power of Attorney

NOTICE: THE POWERS GRANTED BY THIS DOCUMENT ARE BROAD AND SWEEPING. THEY ARE EXPLAINED IN THIS PART. IF YOU HAVE ANY QUESTIONS ABOUT THESE POWERS, OBTAIN COMPETENT LEGAL ADVICE. THIS DOCUMENT DOES NOT AUTHORIZE ANYONE TO MAKE MEDICAL AND OTHER HEALTH CARE DECISIONS FOR YOU. YOU MAY REVOKE THIS POWER OF ATTORNEY IF YOU LATER WISH TO DO SO.

I_____ (name)
_____(address)   do
hereby appoint_____ (name)
_____(address)   as
my agent (attorney-in-fact) to act for me in any lawful way with respect to the following initialed subjects:

TO GRANT ALL OF THE FOLLOWING POWERS, INITIAL THE LINE IN FRONT OF (N) AND IG-NORE THE LINES IN FRONT OF THE OTHER POWERS. TO GRANT ONE OR MORE, BUT FEWER THAN ALL, OF THE FOLLOWING POWERS, INITIAL THE LINE IN FRONT OF EACH POWER YOU ARE GRANTING. TO WITHHOLD A POWER, DO NOT INITIAL THE LINE IN FRONT OF IT. YOU MAY, BUT NEED NOT, CROSS OUT EACH POWER WITHHELD.

INITIAL

_____ (A) real property transactions;

_____ (B) tangible personal property transactions;

_____ (C) stock and bond transactions;

_____ (D) commodity and option transactions;

_____ (E) banking and other financial institution transactions;

_____ (F) business operating transactions;

_____ (G) insurance and annuity transactions;

_____ (H) estate, trust, and other beneficiary transactions;

_____ (I) claims and litigation;

_____ (J) personal and family maintenance;

_____ (K) benefits from social security, medicare, medicaid, or other governmental programs or from military service;

_____ (L) retirement plan transactions;

_____ (M) tax matters;

_____ (N) ALL OF THE POWERS LISTED ABOVE. YOU NEED NOT INITIAL ANY OTHER LINES IF YOU INITIAL LINE (N).

SPECIAL INSTRUCTIONS: ON THE FOLLOWING LINES, YOU MAY GIVE SPECIAL INSTRUCTIONS LIMITING OR EXTENDING THE POWERS GRANTED TO YOUR AGENT.

UNLESS YOU DIRECT OTHERWISE ABOVE, THIS POWER OF ATTORNEY IS EFFECTIVE IMMEDI-ATELY AND WILL CONTINUE UNTIL IT IS REVOKED:

This power of attorney revokes all previous powers of attorney signed by me.

STRIKE THE PRECEDING SENTENCE IF YOU DO NOT WANT THIS POWER OF ATTORNEY TO REVOKE ALL PREVIOUS POWERS OF ATTORNEY SIGNED BY YOU

IF YOU DO WANT THIS POWER OF ATTORNEY TO REVOKE ALL PREVIOUS POWERS OF AT-TORNEY SIGNED BY YOU, YOU SHOULD READ THOSE POWERS OF ATTORNEY AND SATISFY THEIR PROVISIONS CONCERNING REVOCATION. THIRD PARTIES WHO RECEIVED COPIES OF THOSE POWERS OF ATTORNEY SHOULD BE NOTIFIED.

This power of attorney will continue to be effective if I become disabled, incapacitated, or incompetent.

STRIKE THE PRECEDING SENTENCE IF YOU DO NOT WANT THIS POWER OF ATTORNEY TO CONTINUE IF YOU BECOME DISABLED, INCAPACITATED, OR INCOMPETENT.

If it becomes necessary to appoint a conservator of my estate or guardian of my person, I nominate my agent.

STRIKE THE PRECEDING SENTENCE IF YOU DO NOT WANT TO NOMINATE YOUR AGENT AS CONSERVATOR OR GUARDIAN.

If any agent named by me dies, becomes incompetent, resigns or refuses to accept the office of agent, I name the following (each to act alone and successively, in the order named) as successor(s) to the agent:
1._____
2._____

For purposes of this subsection, a person is considered to be incompetent if and while: (1) the person is a minor; (2) the person is an adjudicated incompetent or disabled person; (3) a conservator has been appointed to act for the person; (4) a guardian has been appointed to act for the person; or (5) the person is unable to give prompt and intelligent consideration to business matters as certified by a licensed physician.

I agree that any third party who receives a copy of this document may act under it. I may revoke this power of attorney by a written document that expressly indicates my intent to revoke. Revoca-tion of the power of attorney is not effective as to a third party until the third party learns of the revocation. I agree to indemnify the third party for any claims that arise against the third party because of reliance on this power of attorney.

Signed this_____day of_____, 20_____

_____
(Your Signature)

Notary Acknowledgement

State of _____

(County) of _____

This document was acknowledged before me on_____(Date) by

_____(Name of Principal)

_____

(Signature of Notarial Officer)

_____

Title (and Rank)

(Seal, if any)

[My commission expires:_____]

Acceptance of Appointment by Attorney-in-Fact (Agent)

BY SIGNING, ACCEPTING, OR ACTING UNDER THE APPOINTMENT, THE AGENT ASSUMES THE FIDUCIARY AND OTHER LEGAL RESPONSIBILITIES OF AN AGENT. THE AGENT WORKS EXCLUSIVELY FOR THE BENEFIT OF THE PRINCIPAL. THE FOREMOST DUTY AS THE AGENT IS THAT OF LOYALTY TO AND PROTECTION OF THE BEST INTERESTS OF THE PRINCIPAL. THE AGENT SHALL DIRECT ANY BENEFITS DERIVED FROM THE POWER OF ATTORNEY TO THE PRINCIPAL. THE AGENT HAS A DUTY TO AVOID CONFLICTS OF INTEREST AND TO USE ORDINARY SKILL AND PRUDENCE IN THE EXERCISE OF THESE DUTIES.

_____

(Signature of Agent)

Signed this_____day of _____, 20_____.

Nebraska Durable Power of Attorney

I _____, residing and
domiciled in _____County, Nebraska, Principal, desir-
ing and intending to establish a Power of Attorney operative under the Nebraska Short Form Act,
does hereby appoint, constitute, and designate _____
_____ (name of agent), of or with an office in _____County,
Nebraska, the lawful and true Agent and attorney in fact for Principal; and Principal does hereby
further provide and stipulate in connection therewith as follows:

1. This Power of Attorney is, as marked, a

(   ) Durable Power of Attorney and a
(   ) Contingent Durable Power of Attorney,
upon the contingency of,
(   ) Incompetence of Principal, or
(   ) Other Contingency:_____, or
(   ) Present Durable Power of Attorney
(   ) Nondurable Power of Attorney.

2. By this Power of Attorney, Principal confers upon and grants to Agent plenary power, plenary
power subject to limitations, or all and each of the listed general powers as individually marked:

(   ) Plenary Power; or
(   ) Plenary Power Subject to Limitations, exclusive of General Powers for Domestic and Personal
             Concerns and for Fiduciary Relationships and
(   ) No Other Restrictions, or
(   ) Other Restrictions: _____; or
(   ) General Power for Bank and Financial Transactions.
(   ) General Power for Business Interests.
(   ) General Power for Chattels and Goods.
(   ) General Power for Disputes and Litigation.
(   ) General Power for Domestic and Personal Concerns.
(   ) General Power for Fiduciary Relationships.
(   ) General Power for Governmental and Other Benefits.
(   ) General Power for Insurance Coverages and Policies.
(   ) General Power for Proprietary Interests and Materials.
(   ) General Power for Real Estate.
(   ) General Power for Securities.
(   ) General Power for Records, Reports, and Statements.

3. By this Power of Attorney, Principal makes the following additional provision or provisions:

4. This Power of Attorney revokes and supersedes all prior executed instruments of like import and remains operative until revoked.

EXECUTED AT_____County, Nebraska, on_____, 20____

_____

Signature of Principal

Notary Acknowledgement

State of Nebraska
County of_____)

The foregoing instrument was acknowledged before me on_____, 20____, by the Principal _____.

_____

Signature of Notary Public

New Hampshire Durable Power of Attorney

INFORMATION CONCERNING THE DURABLE POWER OF ATTORNEY. THIS IS AN IMPORTANT LEGAL DOCUMENT. BEFORE SIGNING THIS DOCUMENT YOU SHOULD KNOW THESE IMPORTANT FACTS:

Notice to the Principal: As the ""Principal," you are using this Durable Power of Attorney to grant power to another person (called the "Agent" or "Attorney in Fact") to make decisions, including, but not limited to, decisions concerning your money, property, or both, and to use your money, property, or both on your behalf. If this written Durable Power of Attorney does not limit the powers that you give to your Agent, your Agent will have broad and sweeping powers to sell or otherwise dispose of your property, and to spend your money without advance notice to you or approval by you. Under this document, your agent will continue to have these powers after you become incapacitated, and unless otherwise indicated your Agent will have these powers before you become incapacitated. You have the right to retain this Power and not to release this Power until you instruct your attorney or any other person who may hold this Power of Attorney to so release it to your Agent pursuant to written instructions. You have the right to revoke or take back this Durable Power of Attorney at any time, so long as you are of sound mind. If there is anything about this Durable Power of Attorney that you do not understand, you should seek professional advice.

I _____(name)
of _____(address)
appoint _____ (name)
_____(address)
as my agent (attorney-in-fact) to act for me in any lawful way with respect to the following initialed subjects:

TO GRANT ALL OF THE FOLLOWING POWERS, INITIAL THE LINE IN FRONT OF (N) AND IGNORE THE LINES IN FRONT OF THE OTHER POWERS.

TO GRANT ONE OR MORE, BUT FEWER THAN ALL, OF THE FOLLOWING POWERS, INITIAL THE LINE IN FRONT OF EACH POWER YOU ARE GRANTING.

TO WITHHOLD A POWER, DO NOT INITIAL THE LINE IN FRONT OF IT. YOU MAY, BUT NEED NOT, CROSS OUT EACH POWER WITHHELD.

INITIAL
_____ (A) Real property transactions.
_____ (B) Tangible personal property transactions.
_____ (C) Stock and bond transactions.
_____ (D) Commodity and option transactions.
_____ (E) Banking and other financial institution transactions.

_____ (F) Business operating transactions.

_____ (G) Insurance and annuity transactions.

_____ (H) Estate, trust, and other beneficiary transactions.

_____ (I) Claims and litigation.

_____ (J) Personal and family maintenance.

_____ (K) Benefits from social security, medicare, medicaid, or other governmental programs, or military service.

_____ (L) Retirement plan transactions.

_____ (M) Tax matters.

_____ (N) ALL OF THE POWERS LISTED ABOVE. YOU NEED NOT INITIAL ANY OTHER LINES IF YOU INITIAL LINE (N).

SPECIAL INSTRUCTIONS: HERE YOU MAY GIVE SPECIAL INSTRUCTIONS LIMITING OR EXTENDING THE POWERS GRANTED TO YOUR AGENT.

UNLESS YOU DIRECT OTHERWISE ABOVE, THIS POWER OF ATTORNEY IS EFFECTIVE IMMEDIATELY AND WILL CONTINUE UNTIL IT IS REVOKED.

This power of attorney will continue to be effective even though I become disabled, incapacitated, or incompetent.

STRIKE THE PRECEDING SENTENCE IF YOU DO NOT WANT THIS POWER OF ATTORNEY TO CONTINUE IF YOU BECOME DISABLED, INCAPACITATED, OR INCOMPETENT.

I agree that any third party who receives a copy of this document may act under it. Revocation of the power of attorney is not effective as to a third party until the third party learns of the revocation. I agree to indemnify the third party for any claims that arise against the third party because of reliance on this power of attorney.

Signed this _____ day of _____ , 20_____

_____
Signature of Principal
_____
Social Security Number of Principal

Notary Acknowledgement

State of _____

(County) of _____

This document was acknowledged before me on _____ (Date) by

_____(Name of principal)

_____

(Signature of notarial officer)

(Seal, if any)

_____

(Title (and Rank))

My commission expires: _____

Acceptance of Appointment by Attorney-in-Fact (Agent)

I, _____, have read the attached power of attorney and am the person identified as the Agent for the Principal. I hereby acknowledge that when I act as Agent or ""attorney in fact,"; I am given power under this Durable Power of Attorney to make decisions about money, property, or both belonging to the Principal, and to spend the Principal's money, property, or both on the Principal's behalf, in accordance with the terms of this Durable Power of Attorney. This Durable Power of Attorney is valid only if the Principal is of sound mind when the Principal signs it. When acting in the capacity of Agent, I am under a duty (called a ""fiduciary duty") to observe the standards observed by a prudent person, which means the use of those powers that is reasonable in view of the interests of the Principal and in view of the way in which a person of ordinary judgment would act in carrying out that person's own affairs. If the exercise of my acts is called into question, the burden will be upon me to prove that I acted under the standards of a fiduciary. As the Agent, I am not entitled to use the money or property for my own benefit or to make gifts to myself or others unless the Durable Power of Attorney specifically gives me the authority to do so. As the Agent, my authority under this Durable Power of Attorney will end when the Principal dies and I will not have authority to manage or dispose of any property or administer the estate unless I am authorized to do so by a New Hampshire Probate Court. If I violate my fiduciary duty under this Durable Power of Attorney, I may be liable for damages and may be subject to criminal prosecution. If there is anything about this Durable Power of Attorney, or my duties under it, that I do not understand, I understand that I should seek professional advice.

_____

Signature of Agent

New Mexico Durable Power of Attorney

NOTICE: THIS IS AN IMPORTANT DOCUMENT. THE POWERS GRANTED BY THIS DOCUMENT ARE BROAD AND SWEEPING. THEY ARE EXPLAINED IN THE UNIFORM STATUTORY FORM POWER OF ATTORNEY ACT, CHAPTER 45, ARTICLE 5, PART 6 NMSA 1978. IF YOU HAVE ANY QUESTIONS ABOUT THESE POWERS, YOU SHOULD ASK A LAWYER TO EXPLAIN THEM TO YOU. THIS FORM DOES NOT PROHIBIT THE USE OF ANY OTHER FORM. YOU MAY REVOKE THIS POWER OF ATTORNEY IF YOU LATER WISH TO DO SO.

I, _____ (Name) reside at
_____, (Address) New Mexico.
I appoint _____ (Name)
whos resides at _____,
(Address) to serve as my attorney(s)-in-fact. If any attorney-in-fact appointed above is unable to serve, then I appoint _____ to serve as successor attorney-in-fact in place of the person who is unable to serve. This power of attorney shall not be affected by my incapacity but will terminate upon my death unless I have revoked it prior to my death. I intend by this power of attorney to avoid a court-supervised guardianship or conservatorship. Should my attempt be defeated, I ask that my agent be appointed as guardian or conservator of my person or estate.

STRIKE THROUGH THE SENTENCE ABOVE IF YOU DO NOT WANT TO NOMINATE YOUR AGENT AS YOUR GUARDIAN OR CONSERVATOR.

CHECK AND INITIAL THE FOLLOWING PARAGRAPH ONLY IF YOU WANT YOUR ATTORNEY(S)-IN-FACT TO BE ABLE TO ACT ALONE AND INDEPENDENTLY OF EACH OTHER. IF YOU DO NOT CHECK AND INITIAL THE FOLLOWING PARAGRAPH AND MORE THAN ONE PERSON IS NAMED TO ACT ON YOUR BEHALF THEN THEY MUST ACT JOINTLY.

(   ) If more than one person is appointed to serve as my attorney-in-fact then they may act severally, alone and independently of each other._____

My attorney(s)-in-fact shall have the power to act in my name, place and stead in any way which I myself could do with respect to the following matters to the extent permitted by law:

INITIAL IN THE BOX IN FRONT OF EACH AUTHORIZATION WHICH YOU DESIRE TO GIVE TO YOUR ATTORNEY(S)-IN-FACT. YOUR ATTORNEY(S)-IN-FACT SHALL BE AUTHORIZED TO ENGAGE ONLY IN THOSE ACTIVITIES WHICH ARE INITIALED.

INITIAL
(____) 1. real estate transactions.
(____) 2. stock and bond transactions.
(____) 3. commodity and option transactions.
(____) 4. tangible personal property transactions.
(____) 5. banking and other financial institution transactions.

(_____) 6. business operating transactions.

(_____) 7. insurance and annuity transactions.

(_____) 8. estate, trust and other beneficiary transactions.

(_____) 9. claims and litigation.

(_____) 10. personal and family maintenance.

(_____) 11. benefits from social security, medicare, medicaid or other government programs or civil or military service.

(_____) 12. retirement plan transactions.

(_____) 13. tax matters, including any transactions with the Internal Revenue Service.

(_____) 14. decisions regarding lifesaving and life prolonging medical treatment.

(_____) 15. decisions relating to medical treatment, surgical treatment, nursing care, medication, hospitalization, institutionalization in a nursing home or other facility and home health care.

(_____) 16. transfer of property or income as a gift to the principal's spouse for the purpose of qualifying the principal for governmental medical assistance.

(_____) 17. ALL OF THE ABOVE POWERS, INCLUDING FINANCIAL AND HEALTH CARE DECISIONS. IF YOU INITIAL THE BOX IN FRONT OF LINE 17, YOU NEED NOT INITIAL ANY OTHER LINES.

SPECIAL INSTRUCTIONS: IN THE FOLLOWING SPACE YOU MAY GIVE SPECIAL INSTRUCTIONS LIMITING OR EXTENDING THE POWERS YOU HAVE GRANTED TO YOUR AGENT.

CHECK AND INITIAL THE FOLLOWING PARAGRAPH IF YOU INTEND FOR THIS POWER OF AT-TORNEY TO BECOME EFFECTIVE ONLY IF YOU BECOME INCAPACITATED. YOUR FAILURE TO DO SO WILL MEAN THAT YOUR ATTORNEY(S)-IN-FACT ARE EMPOWERED TO ACT ON YOUR BEHALF FROM THE TIME YOU SIGN THIS DOCUMENT UNTIL YOUR DEATH UNLESS YOU REVOKE THE POWER BEFORE YOUR DEATH.

(   ) (Check Here) _____ (Initial Here) This power of attorney shall become effective only if I become incapacitated. My attorney(s)-in-fact shall be entitled to rely on notarized statements from two qualified health care professionals, one of whom shall be a physician, as to my incapacity. By incapacity I mean that among other things, I am unable to effectively manage my personal care, property or financial affairs.

This power of attorney will not be affected by lapse of time. I agree that any third party who receives a copy of this power of attorney may act under it.

_____

(Signature)

_____

(Optional, but preferred: Your social security number)

Dated:_____, 20_____

Notary Acknowledgement

NOTICE: IF THIS POWER OF ATTORNEY AFFECTS REAL ESTATE, IT MUST BE RECORDED IN THE OFFICE OF THE COUNTY CLERK IN EACH COUNTY WHERE THE REAL ESTATE IS LOCATED.

STATE OF NEW MEXICO) ss.

COUNTY OF _____)

The foregoing instrument was acknowledged before me on _____, 20_____,

by _____.

_____.

Notary Public

My Commission Expires: _____

BY ACCEPTING OR ACTING UNDER THE POWER OF ATTORNEY, YOUR AGENT ASSUMES THE FIDUCIARY AND OTHER LEGAL RESPONSIBILITIES OF AN AGENT ACTING ON YOUR BEHALF." and "THIS AFFIDAVIT IS FOR THE USE OF YOUR ATTORNEY(S)-IN-FACT IF EVER YOUR ATTORNEY(S)-IN-FACT ACTS ON YOUR BEHALF UNDER YOUR WRITTEN POWER OF ATTORNEY.

AFFIDAVIT AS TO POWER OF ATTORNEY BEING IN FULL FORCE

STATE OF NEW MEXICO) ss.

COUNTY OF _____)

I/we _____ being duly sworn, state:

1. _____ ("Principal") of

_____ County, New Mexico, signed a written Power

of Attorney on _____, 20_____, appointing the undersigned as his/her attorney(s)-in-fact. (A true copy of the power of attorney is attached hereto and incorporated herein.)

2. As attorney(s)-in-fact and under and by virtue of the Power of Attorney, I/we have this date executed the following described instrument: _____

3. At the time of executing the above described instrument I/we had no actual knowledge or actual notice of revocation or termination of the Power of Attorney by death or otherwise, or notice of any facts indicating the same.

4. I/we represent that the principal is now alive; has not, at any time, revoked or repudiated the power of attorney; and the power of attorney still is in full force and effect.

5. I/we make this affidavit for the purpose of inducing _____

to accept delivery of the above described instrument, as executed by me/us in my/our capacity of attorney(s)-in-fact for the Principal.

_____, Attorney-in-fact

_____, Attorney-in-fact

Sworn to before me _____ this _____ day

of _____, 20_____.

_____

Notary Public

My Commission Expires: _____

New York Durable Power of Attorney

THE POWERS YOU GRANT BELOW CONTINUE TO BE EFFECTIVE SHOULD YOU BECOME DISABLED OR INCOMPETENT

CAUTION: THIS IS AN IMPORTANT DOCUMENT. IT GIVES THE PERSON WHOM YOU DESIGNATE (YOUR "AGENT") BROAD POWERS TO HANDLE YOUR PROPERTY DURING YOUR LIFETIME, WHICH MAY INCLUDE POWERS TO MORTGAGE, SELL, OR OTHERWISE DISPOSE OF ANY REAL OR PERSONAL PROPERTY WITHOUT ADVANCE NOTICE TO YOU OR APPROVAL BY YOU. THESE POWERS WILL CONTINUE TO EXIST EVEN AFTER YOU BECOME DISABLED OR INCOMPETENT. THESE POWERS ARE EXPLAINED MORE FULLY IN NEW YORK GENERAL OBLIGATIONS LAW, ARTICLE 5, TITLE 15, SECTIONS 5-1502A THROUGH 5-1503, WHICH EXPRESSLY PERMIT THE USE OF ANY OTHER OR DIFFERENT FORM OF POWER OF ATTORNEY. THIS DOCUMENT DOES NOT AUTHORIZE ANYONE TO MAKE MEDICAL OR OTHER HEALTH CARE DECISIONS. YOU MAY EXECUTE A HEALTH CARE PROXY TO DO THIS. IF THERE IS ANYTHING ABOUT THIS FORM THAT YOU DO NOT UNDERSTAND, YOU SHOULD ASK A LAWYER TO EXPLAIN IT TO YOU.

THIS is intended to constitute a DURABLE GENERAL POWER OF ATTORNEY pursuant to Article 5, Title 15 of the New York General Obligations Law:

I,_____,
of _____,
(insert your name and address) do hereby appoint:_____,
of _____,
(If one person is to be appointed agent, insert the name and address of your agent)

_____,
of_____,
(If 2 or more persons are to be appointed agents by you insert their names and addresses above)

my attorney(s)-in-fact TO ACT
(If more than one agent is designated, CHOOSE ONE of the following two choices by putting your initials in ONE of the blank spaces to the left of your choice:)
(   ) Each agent may SEPARATELY act.
(   ) All agents must act TOGETHER.
(If neither blank space is initialed, the agents will be required to act TOGETHER)

IN MY NAME, PLACE AND STEAD in any way which I myself could do, if I were personally present, with respect to the following matters as each of them is defined in Title 15 of Article 5 of the New York General Obligations Law to the extent that I am permitted by law to act through an agent:
(DIRECTIONS: Initial in the blank space to the left of your choice any one or more of the following lettered subdivisions as to which you WANT to give your agent authority. If the blank space to the left of any particular lettered subdivision is NOT initialed, NO AUTHORITY WILL BE GRANTED for matters that are included in that subdivision. Alternatively, the letter corresponding to each power you wish to grant may be written or typed on the blank line in subdivision "(Q)", and you may then put your initials in

118

the blank space to the left of subdivision "(Q)" in order to grant each of the powers so indicated)

(   ) (A) real estate transactions;
(   ) (B) chattel and goods transactions;
(   ) (C) bond, share and commodity transactions;
(   ) (D) banking transactions;
(   ) (E) business operating transactions;
(   ) (F) insurance transactions;
(   ) (G) estate transactions;
(   ) (H) claims and litigation;
(   ) (I) personal relationships and affairs;
(   ) (J) benefits from military service;
(   ) (K) records, reports and statements;
(   ) (L) retirement benefit transactions;
(   ) (M) making gifts to my spouse, children and more remote descendants, and parents, not to exceed in the aggregate $10,000 to each of such persons in any year;
(   ) (N) tax matters;
(   ) (O) all other matters;
(   ) (P) full and unqualified authority to my attorney(s)-in-fact to delegate any or all of the foregoing powers to any person or persons whom my attorney(s)-in-fact shall select;
(   ) (Q) each of the above matters identified by the following letters:_____.

(Special provisions and limitations may be included in the statutory short form durable power of attorney only if they conform to he requirements of section 5-1503 of the New York General Obligations Law.)

This durable Power of Attorney shall not be affected by my subsequent disability or incompetence.

If every agent named above is unable or unwilling to serve, I appoint

_____,
of _____,
(insert name and address of successor)
to be my agent for all purposes hereunder.

TO INDUCE ANY THIRD PARTY TO ACT HEREUNDER, I HEREBY AGREE THAT ANY   THIRD PARTY RECEIV-ING A DULY EXECUTED COPY OR FACSIMILE OF THIS   INSTRUMENT MAY ACT HEREUNDER, AND THAT REVOCATION OR TERMINATION HEREOF SHALL BE INEFFECTIVE AS TO SUCH THIRD PARTY UNLESS AND UNTIL ACTUAL NOTICE OR KNOWLEDGE OF SUCH REVOCATION OR TERMINATION SHALL HAVE BEEN RECEIVED BY SUCH THIRD PARTY, AND I FOR MYSELF AND FOR MY HEIRS, EXECUTORS, LEGAL REPRESENTATIVES AND ASSIGNS, HEREBY AGREE TO INDEMNIFY AND HOLD HARMLESS ANY SUCH THIRD PARTY FROM AND AGAINST ANY AND ALL CLAIMS THAT MAY ARISE AGAINST SUCH THIRD PARTY BY REASON OF SUCH THIRD PARTY HAVING RELIED ON THE PROVISIONS OF THIS INSTRUMENT.

THIS DURABLE GENERAL POWER OF ATTORNEY MAY BE REVOKED BY ME AT ANY TIME.

In Witness Whereof I have hereunto signed my name this _____ day of _____ 20_____.

_____.
(Signature of Principal)

Notary Acknowledgement

STATE OF NEW YORK
COUNTY OF _____

On this _____ day of _____, 20_____ before me the undersigned, personally appeared ,_____, personally known to be or proved to me on the basis of satisfactory evidence to be the individual whose name is subscribed to the within instrument and acknowledged to me that he executed the same in his capacity, and that by his signature on the instrument, the individual, or the person who acted on behalf of the individual, executed the instrument and that such individual made such appearance before the undersigned in the City of _____, County of _____, State of New York.

_____
Notary Signature

North Carolina Durable Power of Attorney

"NOTICE: THE POWERS GRANTED BY THIS DOCUMENT ARE BROAD AND SWEEPING. THEY ARE DEFINED IN CHAPTER 32A OF THE NORTH CAROLINA GENERAL STATUTES WHICH EXPRESSLY PERMITS THE USE OF ANY OTHER OR DIFFERENT FORM OF POWER OF ATTORNEY DESIRED BY THE PARTIES CONCERNED.

State of _____

County of _____

I _____, appoint
_____ to be my
attorney-in-fact, to act in my name in any way which I could act for myself, with respect to the following matters as each of them is defined in Chapter 32A of the North Carolina General Statutes.
(DIRECTIONS: Initial the line opposite any one or more of the subdivisions as to which the principal desires to give the attorney-in-fact authority.)

(1)...... Real property transactions   _____
(2)...... Personal property transactions   _____
(3)...... Bond, share, stock, securities and commodity transactions   _____
(4)   Banking transactions   _____
(5)...... Safe deposits   _____
(6)...... Business operating transactions   _____
(7)...... Insurance transactions   _____
(8)...... Estate transactions.   _____
(9)...... Personal relationships and affairs   _____
(10).... Social security and unemployment.   _____
(11).... Benefits from military service.   _____
(12).... Tax matters   _____
(13).... Employment of agents.   _____
(14).... Gifts to charities, and to individuals other than the attorney-in-fact   _____
(15).... Gifts to the named attorney-in-fact   _____

(If power of substitution and revocation is to be given, initial the following sentence:

_____I also give to such person full power to appoint another to act as my attorney-in-fact and full power to revoke such appointment.

(If period of power of attorney is to be limited, initial the following sentence:

_____This power terminates _____, 20_____

If power of attorney is to be a durable power of attorney under the provision of Article

2 of Chapter 32A and is to continue in effect after the incapacity or mental incompetence of the principal, initial the following sentence:

_____This power of attorney shall not be affected by my subsequent incapacity or mental incompetence.

If power of attorney is to take effect only after the incapacity or mental incompetence of the principal, initial this sentence.

_____This power of attorney shall become effective after I become incapacitated or mentally incompetent.

If power of attorney is to be effective to terminate or direct the administration of a custodial trust created under the Uniform Custodial Trust Act, initial the following sentence:

_____In the event of my subsequent incapacity or mental incompetence, the attorney-in-fact of this power of attorney shall have the power to terminate or to direct the administration of any custodial trust of which I am the beneficiary.

If power of attorney is to be effective to determine whether a beneficiary under the Uniform Custodial Trust Act is incapacitated or ceases to be incapacitated, initial the following sentence:

_____The attorney-in-fact of this power of attorney shall have the power to determine whether I am incapacitated or whether my incapacity has ceased for the purposes of any custodial trust of which I am the beneficiary.

Dated_____, 20_____ .

_____
Signature of Principal

Notary Acknowledgement

STATE OF _____
COUNTY OF _____
On this _____ day of_____, 20_____, personally appeared before me, the said named
_____ to me known and
known to me to be the person described in and who executed the foregoing instrument and he (or she) acknowledged that he (or she) executed the same and being duly sworn by me, made oath that the statements in the foregoing instrument are true.

_____   My Commission Expires _____
(Signature of Notary Public)

Oklahoma Durable Power of Attorney

NOTICE: THE POWERS GRANTED BY THIS DOCUMENT ARE BROAD AND SWEEPING. THEY ARE EXPLAINED IN THE UNIFORM STATUTORY FORM POWER OF ATTORNEY ACT. IF YOU HAVE ANY QUESTIONS ABOUT THESE POWERS, OBTAIN COMPETENT LEGAL ADVICE. THIS DOCUMENT DOES NOT AUTHORIZE ANYONE TO MAKE MEDICAL AND OTHER HEALTH-CARE DECISIONS FOR YOU. YOU MAY REVOKE THIS POWER OF ATTORNEY IF YOU LATER WISH TO DO SO.

I _____(name)
of _____(address)
appoint _____ (name)
_____(address)
as my agent (attorney-in-fact) to act for me in any lawful way with respect to the following initialed subjects:

TO GRANT ALL OF THE FOLLOWING POWERS, INITIAL THE LINE IN FRONT OF (N) AND IGNORE THE LINES IN FRONT OF THE OTHER POWERS.

TO GRANT ONE OR MORE, BUT FEWER THAN ALL, OF THE FOLLOWING POWERS, INITIAL THE LINE IN FRONT OF EACH POWER YOU ARE GRANTING.

TO WITHHOLD A POWER, DO NOT INITIAL THE LINE IN FRONT OF IT. YOU MAY, BUT NEED NOT, CROSS OUT EACH POWER WITHHELD.

INITIAL
_____ (A) Real property transactions.
_____ (B) Tangible personal property transactions.
_____ (C) Stock and bond transactions.
_____ (D) Commodity and option transactions.
_____ (E) Banking and other financial institution transactions.
_____ (F) Business operating transactions.
_____ (G) Insurance and annuity transactions.
_____ (H) Estate, trust, and other beneficiary transactions.
_____ (I) Claims and litigation.
_____ (J) Personal and family maintenance.
_____ (K) Benefits from social security, medicare, medicaid, or other governmental programs, or military service.
_____ (L) Retirement plan transactions.
_____ (M) Tax matters.
_____ (N) ALL OF THE POWERS LISTED ABOVE. YOU NEED NOT INITIAL ANY OTHER LINES IF YOU INITIAL LINE (N).

SPECIAL INSTRUCTIONS: HERE YOU MAY GIVE SPECIAL INSTRUCTIONS LIMITING OR EXTENDING THE POWERS GRANTED TO YOUR AGENT:

UNLESS YOU DIRECT OTHERWISE ABOVE, THIS POWER OF ATTORNEY IS EFFECTIVE IMMEDIATELY AND WILL CONTINUE UNTIL IT IS REVOKED.

This power of attorney will continue to be effective even though I become disabled, incapacitated, or incompetent.

STRIKE THE PRECEDING SENTENCE IF YOU DO NOT WANT THIS POWER OF ATTORNEY TO CONTINUE IF YOU BECOME DISABLED, INCAPACITATED, OR INCOMPETENT.

I agree that any third party who receives a copy of this document may act under it. Revocation of the power of attorney is not effective as to a third party until the third party learns of the revocation. I agree to indemnify the third party for any claims that arise against the third party because of reliance on this power of attorney.

Signed this _____ day of _____ , 20_____

_____
Signature of Principal

_____
City, County, and State of Residence

Witness Attestation

The principal is personally known to me and I believe the principal to be of sound mind. I am eighteen (18) years of age or older. I am not related to the principal by blood or marriage, or related to the attorney-in-fact by blood or marriage. The principal has declared to me that this instrument is his power of attorney granting to the named attorney-in-fact the power and authority specified herein, and that he has willingly made and executed it as his free and voluntary act for the purposes herein expressed.

First Witness Signature:_____

Second Witness Signature:_____

Notary Acknowledgement

STATE OF OKLAHOMA   ) SS.
COUNTY OF_____)

Before me, the undersigned authority, on this ____ day of _____, 20____, personally appeared _____ (principal), _____ (witness), and _____ (witness), whose names are subscribed to the foregoing instrument in their respective capacities, and all of said persons being by me duly sworn, the principal declared to me and to the said witnesses in my presence that the instrument is his or her power of attorney, and that the principal has willingly and voluntarily made and executed it as the free act and deed of the principal for the purposes therein expressed, and the witnesses declared to me that they were each eighteen (18) years of age or over, and that neither of them is related to the principal by blood or marriage, or related to the attorney-in-fact by blood or marriage.

_____
Notary Public Signature   My Commission Expires:

Pennsylvania Durable Power of Attorney

NOTICE: THE PURPOSE OF THIS POWER OF ATTORNEY IS TO GIVE THE PERSON YOU DESIGNATE (YOUR "AGENT") BROAD POWERS TO HANDLE YOUR PROPERTY, WHICH MAY INCLUDE POWERS TO SELL OR OTHERWISE DISPOSE OF ANY REAL OR PERSONAL PROPERTY WITHOUT ADVANCE NOTICE TO YOU OR APPROVAL BY YOU. THIS POWER OF ATTORNEY DOES NOT IMPOSE A DUTY ON YOUR AGENT TO EXERCISE GRANTED POWERS, BUT WHEN POWERS ARE EXERCISED, YOUR AGENT MUST USE DUE CARE TO ACT FOR YOUR BENEFIT AND IN ACCORDANCE WITH THIS POWER OF ATTORNEY. YOUR AGENT MAY EXERCISE THE POWERS GIVEN HERE THROUGHOUT YOUR LIFETIME, EVEN AFTER YOU BECOME INCAPACITATED, UNLESS YOU EXPRESSLY LIMIT THE DURATION OF THESE POWERS OR YOU REVOKE THESE POWERS OR A COURT ACTING ON YOUR BEHALF TERMINATES YOUR AGENT'S AUTHORITY. YOUR AGENT MUST KEEP YOUR FUNDS SEPARATE FROM YOUR AGENT'S FUNDS. A COURT CAN TAKE AWAY THE POWERS OF YOUR AGENT IF IT FINDS YOUR AGENT IS NOT ACTING PROPERLY. THE POWERS AND DUTIES OF AN AGENT UNDER A POWER OF ATTORNEY ARE EXPLAINED MORE FULLY IN 20 PA.C.S. CH. 56. IF THERE IS ANYTHING ABOUT THIS FORM THAT YOU DO NOT UNDERSTAND, YOU SHOULD ASK A LAWYER OF YOUR OWN CHOOSING TO EXPLAIN IT TO YOU.

I HAVE READ OR HAD EXPLAINED TO ME THIS NOTICE AND I UNDERSTAND ITS CONTENTS.

_____   _____

(Signature of Principal)   (Date)

NOTICE: THE POWERS GRANTED BY THIS DOCUMENT ARE BROAD AND SWEEPING. THEY ARE EXPLAINED IN THE UNIFORM STATUTORY FORM POWER OF ATTORNEY ACT. IF YOU HAVE ANY QUESTIONS ABOUT THESE POWERS, OBTAIN COMPETENT LEGAL ADVICE. THIS DOCUMENT DOES NOT AUTHORIZE ANYONE TO MAKE MEDICAL AND OTHER HEALTH-CARE DECISIONS FOR YOU. YOU MAY REVOKE THIS POWER OF ATTORNEY IF YOU LATER WISH TO DO SO.

I _____ (name)
of _____ (address)
appoint _____ (name)
_____ (address)
as my agent (attorney-in-fact) to act for me in any lawful way with respect to the following initialed subjects:

TO GRANT ALL OF THE FOLLOWING POWERS, INITIAL THE LINE IN FRONT OF (N) AND IGNORE THE LINES IN FRONT OF THE OTHER POWERS.
TO GRANT ONE OR MORE, BUT FEWER THAN ALL, OF THE FOLLOWING POWERS, INITIAL THE LINE IN FRONT OF EACH POWER YOU ARE GRANTING.
TO WITHHOLD A POWER, DO NOT INITIAL THE LINE IN FRONT OF IT. YOU MAY, BUT NEED NOT, CROSS OUT EACH POWER WITHHELD.

INITIAL
_____ (A) Real property transactions.
_____ (B) Tangible personal property transactions.
_____ (C) Stock and bond transactions.

_____ (D) Commodity and option transactions.

_____ (E) Banking and other financial institution transactions.

_____ (F) Business operating transactions.

_____ (G) Insurance and annuity transactions.

_____ (H) Estate, trust, and other beneficiary transactions.

_____ (I) Claims and litigation.

_____ (J) Personal and family maintenance.

_____ (K) Benefits from social security, medicare, medicaid, or other governmental programs, or military service.

_____ (L) Retirement plan transactions.

_____ (M) Tax matters.

_____ (N) ALL OF THE POWERS LISTED ABOVE. YOU NEED NOT INITIAL ANY OTHER LINES IF YOU INITIAL LINE (N).

SPECIAL INSTRUCTIONS: HERE YOU MAY GIVE SPECIAL INSTRUCTIONS LIMITING OR EXTENDING THE POWERS GRANTED TO YOUR AGENT:

UNLESS YOU DIRECT OTHERWISE ABOVE, THIS POWER OF ATTORNEY IS EFFECTIVE IMMEDIATELY AND WILL CONTINUE UNTIL IT IS REVOKED.

This power of attorney will continue to be effective even though I become disabled, incapacitated, or incompetent.

STRIKE THE PRECEDING SENTENCE IF YOU DO NOT WANT THIS POWER OF ATTORNEY TO CONTINUE IF YOU BECOME DISABLED, INCAPACITATED, OR INCOMPETENT.

I agree that any third party who receives a copy of this document may act under it. Revocation of the power of attorney is not effective as to a third party until the third party learns of the revocation. I agree to indemnify the third party for any claims that arise against the third party because of reliance on this power of attorney.

Signed this _____ day of _____ , 20_____

_____
Signature of Principal

_____
City, County, and State of Residence

Acknowledgment executed by agent.--An agent shall have no authority to act as agent under the power of attorney unless the agent has first executed and affixed to the power of attorney an acknowledgment in substantially the following form:

I, _____ (printed name of agent), have read the attached power of attorney and am the person identified as the agent for the principal. I hereby acknowledge that in the absence of a specific provision to the contrary in the power of attorney or in 20 Pa.C.S. when I act as agent:

I shall exercise the powers for the benefit of the principal.

I shall keep the assets of the principal separate from my assets.

I shall exercise reasonable caution and prudence.

I shall keep a full and accurate record of all actions, receipts and disbursements on behalf of the principal.

_____   _____

(Agent signature)   (Date)

Rhode Island Durable Power of Attorney

NOTICE: This is an important legal document which is authorized by the general laws of this state. The powers granted by this document are broad and sweeping. They are defined in §§ 18-16-1 to 18-16-12, both inclusive, of the general laws in chapter 18-16 entitled "Rhode Island Short Form Power of Attorney Act." The use of the short form power of attorney is strictly voluntary, and chapter 18-16 specifically authorizes the use of any other or different form of power of attorney upon mutual agreement of the parties concerned.

Known All Men by These Presents, which are intended to constitute a GENERAL POWER OF ATTORNEY pursuant to the Rhode Island Short Form Power of Attorney Act:

That   I_____

_____
(insert name and address of the principal) do hereby appoint

_____

_____
(insert name and address of the agent, or each agent, if more than one is designated)

my attorney(s)-in-fact TO ACT_____.

(If more than one agent is designated and the principal wishes each agent alone to be able to exercise the power conferred, insert in this blank the word "severally". Failure to make any insertion or the insertion of the word "jointly" shall require the agents to act jointly.)

First: In my name, place and stead in any way which I myself could do, if I were personally present, with respect to the following matters as each of them is defined in the Rhode Island Statutory Short Form Power of Attorney Act to the extent that I am permitted by law to act through an agent:

(STRIKE OUT AND INITIAL ON THE OPPOSITE LINE ANY ONE OR MORE OF THE SUBDIVISIONS AS TO WHICH THE PRINCIPAL DOES NOT DESIRE TO GIVE THE AGENT AUTHORITY. SUCH ELIMINATION OF ANY ONE OR MORE OF SUBDIVISIONS (A) TO (I), INCLUSIVE, SHALL AUTOMATICALLY CONSTITUTE AN ELIMINATION ALSO OF SUBDIVISION (J).

To strike out any subdivision the principal must draw a line through the text of that subdivision AND write his initials in the line opposite.

INITIAL

_____   (A) real state transactions;

_____   (B) chattel and goods transactions;

_____   (C) bond, share and commodity transactions;

_____   (D) banking transactions;

_____ (E) business operating transactions;
_____ (F) insurance transactions;
_____ (G) (claims and litigations;
_____ (H) benefits from military service;
_____ (I) records, reports and statements;
_____ (J) all other matters;

(Special provisions and limitations may be included in the statutory short form power of attorney only if they conform to the requirements of the Rhode Island Statutory Short Form Power of Attorney Act.)

Strike though either (A) or (B) below:
Second: This power of attorney shall:
(A) be of indefinite duration or
(B) terminate on the following date, _____, unless otherwise terminated by revocation, destruction or other affirmative action.

Third: Hereby ratifying and confirming all that said attorney(s) or substitute(s) do or cause to be done.

In witness whereof I have hereunto signed my name and affixed my seal this _____ day of
_____ 20_____.
_____ (Signature of Principal)

Notary Acknowledgement
State of Rhode Island   County of _____
This document was acknowledged before me on _____ (Date) by
_____ (name of principal)
_____   Seal) _____
Signature of Notary Public)   My commission expires: _____

If you selected "A" above, and if you wish to have this power of attorney be effective even if you are incompetent, you must also sign below and have this second signature also notarized.

This power of attorney shall not be affected by the subsequent incompetency of the donor.
In witness whereof I have hereunto signed my name and affixed my seal this _____ day of
_____ 20_____.
_____ (Signature of Principal)

Notary Acknowledgement
State of Rhode Island   County of _____
This document was acknowledged before me on _____ (Date) by
_____ (name of principal)
_____   Seal
Signature of Notary Public)   My commission expires: _____

Texas Durable Power of Attorney

NOTICE: THE POWERS GRANTED BY THIS DOCUMENT ARE BROAD AND SWEEPING. THEY ARE EXPLAINED IN THE DURABLE POWER OF ATTORNEY ACT, CHAPTER XII, TEXAS PROBATE CODE. IF YOU HAVE ANY QUESTIONS ABOUT THESE POWERS, OBTAIN COMPETENT LEGAL ADVICE. THIS DOCUMENT DOES NOT AUTHORIZE ANYONE TO MAKE MEDICAL AND OTHER HEALTH-CARE DECISIONS FOR YOU. YOU MAY REVOKE THIS POWER OF ATTORNEY IF YOU LATER WISH TO DO SO.

I, _____

(insert your name and address), appoint

_____

(insert the name and address of the person appointed) as my agent (attorney-in-fact) to act for me in any lawful way with respect to all of the following powers except for a power that I have crossed out below.

TO WITHHOLD A POWER, YOU MUST CROSS OUT EACH POWER WITHHELD.

> Real property transactions;
> Tangible personal property transactions;
> Stock and bond transactions;
> Commodity and option transactions;
> Banking and other financial institution transactions;
> Business operating transactions;
> Insurance and annuity transactions;
> Estate, trust, and other beneficiary transactions;
> Claims and litigation;
> Personal and family maintenance;
> Benefits from social security, Medicare, Medicaid, or other governmental programs or civil or military service;
> Retirement plan transactions;
> Tax matters.

IF NO POWER LISTED ABOVE IS CROSSED OUT, THIS DOCUMENT SHALL BE CONSTRUED AND INTERPRETED AS A GENERAL POWER OF ATTORNEY AND MY AGENT (ATTORNEY IN FACT) SHALL HAVE THE POWER AND AUTHORITY TO PERFORM OR UNDERTAKE ANY ACTION I COULD PERFORM OR UNDERTAKE IF I WERE PERSONALLY PRESENT.

Special instructions applicable to gifts (initial in front of the following sentence to have it apply):

_____ I grant my agent (attorney in fact) the power to apply my property to make gifts, except that the amount of a gift to an individual may not exceed the amount of annual exclusions allowed from the federal gift tax for the calendar year of the gift.

ON THE FOLLOWING LINES YOU MAY GIVE SPECIAL INSTRUCTIONS LIMITING OR EXTENDING THE POWERS GRANTED TO YOUR AGENT.

UNLESS YOU DIRECT OTHERWISE ABOVE, THIS POWER OF ATTORNEY IS EFFECTIVE IMMEDIATELY AND WILL CONTINUE UNTIL IT IS REVOKED. CHOOSE ONE OF THE FOLLOWING ALTERNATIVES BY CROSSING OUT THE ALTERNATIVE NOT CHOSEN:

(A) This power of attorney is not affected by my subsequent disability or incapacity.

(B) This power of attorney becomes effective upon my disability or incapacity.

YOU SHOULD CHOOSE ALTERNATIVE (A) IF THIS POWER OF ATTORNEY IS TO BECOME EFFECTIVE ON THE DATE IT IS EXECUTED. IF NEITHER (A) NOR (B) IS CROSSED OUT, IT WILL BE ASSUMED THAT YOU CHOSE ALTERNATIVE (A).

If Alternative (B) is chosen and a definition of my disability or incapacity is not contained in this power of attorney, I shall be considered disabled or incapacitated for purposes of this power of attorney if a physician certifies in writing at a date later than the date this power of attorney is executed that, based on the physician's medical examination of me, I am mentally incapable of managing my financial affairs. I authorize the physician who examines me for this purpose to disclose my physical or mental condition to another person for purposes of this power of attorney. A third party who accepts this power of attorney is fully protected from any action taken under this power of attorney that is based on the determination made by a physician of my disability or incapacity. I agree that any third party who receives a copy of this document may act under it. Revocation of the durable power of attorney is not effective as to a third party until the third party receives actual notice of the revocation. I agree to indemnify the third party for any claims that arise against the third party because of reliance on this power of attorney. If any agent named by me dies, becomes legally disabled, resigns, or refuses to act, I name the following (each to act alone and successively, in the order named) as successor(s) to that agent: _____.

Signed this _____ day of _____, 20____

_____
(signature of principal)

Notary Acknowledgement

State of _____
County of _____

This document was acknowledged before me on _____(date) by

_____.

_____
(Signature of Notarial Officer)   SEAL, if any, of notary
My commission expires: _____

THE ATTORNEY IN FACT OR AGENT, BY ACCEPTING OR ACTING UNDER THE APPOINTMENT, ASSUMES THE FIDUCIARY AND OTHER LEGAL RESPONSIBILITIES OF AN AGENT.

CHAPTER 10
Advance Health Care Directives

What is an Advance Health Care Directive?

An advance health care directive is a legal document that may be used in any state and that allows you to provide written directions relating to your future health care should you become incapacitated and unable to speak for yourself. Advance health care directives give you a direct voice in medical decisions in situations when you cannot make those decisions yourself. Your advance health care directive will not be used as long as you are able to express your own decisions. You can always accept or refuse medical treatment and you always have the legal right to revoke your advance health care directive at any time. Instructions regarding revocations are discussed later in these instructions. The Federal Patient Self-Determination Act encourages all people to make their own decisions about the type of medical care they wish to receive. This act also requires all health care agencies (hospitals, long-term care facilities, and home health agencies) receiving Medicare and Medicaid reimbursement to recognize a living will and health care power of attorney as advance directives. Under this Act, all health care agencies must ask you if you have advance directives and must give you materials with information about your rights under state law.

Advance health care directives are not only for senior citizens. Serious life-threatening accidents or disease can strike anyone and leave them unable to communicate their desires. In fact, the rise of the use of advance health care directives can be attributed in part, to legal cases involving medical care to young people, particularly Karen Ann Quinlan and Nancy Cruzan, and most recently, Terry Schiavo. Anyone over the age of 18 (19 in Alabama) who is mentally competent should complete an advance health care directive. Be aware, however, that advance health care directives are intended for non-emergency medical treatment. Most often, there is no time for health care providers to consult and analyze the provisions of an advance health care directive in an emergency situation.

The advance health care directives that are contained on the cd that is enclosed with this book all contain four separate sections, each dealing with different aspects of potential situations that may arise during a possible period of incapacitation:

- Living will
- Selection of health care agent (generally, by health care power of attorney)
- Designation of primary physician
- Organ donation

In addition, this book also provides (in Chapter 6) a fifth legal form that may be useful in many health care situations if you are unable to handle your own financial affairs: a durable unlimited power of attorney for financial affairs. A brief explanation of each of these forms follows:

Living Will: A *living will* is a document that can be used to state your desire that extraordinary life support means not be used to artificially prolong your life in the event that you are stricken with a terminal disease or injury. Its use has been recognized in all states in recent years. The purpose of a living will is to provide doctors and other health care workers with clear directions regarding how you would like your medical care handled toward the end of your life. A living will makes it possible for you to specify, in advance, exactly what your preferences are regarding the use of life-sustaining medical procedures if you are ever in a terminal medical condition or in a vegetative state, and are unable to give such directions yourself.

Health Care Power of Attorney: This relatively new legal document has been developed to allow a person to appoint another person to make health care decisions on one's behalf, in the event that he or she becomes incapacitated or incompetent. Generally, a *health care power of attorney* will only take effect upon a person becoming unable to manage his or her own affairs, and only after this incapacitation has been certified by an attending physician. The person appointed will then have the authority to view your medical records, consult with your doctors and make any required decisions regarding your health care. This document may be carefully tailored to fit your needs and concerns and can be used in conjunction with a living will. It can be a valuable tool for dealing with difficult healthcare situations. For instructions and forms for preparing an individual durable health care power of attorney that is not part of an advance health care directive, please refer to Chapter 7.

Designation of Primary Physician: Through the use of this document, you will be able to designate your choice for your primary physician in the event you are unable to communicate your wishes after an accident or during an illness. Although your family may know your personal doctor, it may still be a good idea to put this choice in writing so that there is no question regarding who your choice for a doctor may be.

Organ Donation: You may also wish that your vital organs or, indeed, your entire body be used after your death for various medical purposes. Every year, many lives are saved and much medical research is enhanced by organ donations. All states allow for you to personally declare your desires regarding the use of your body and/or organs after death.

Durable Unlimited Power of Attorney for Financial Affairs: Situations may arise when you are unable to handle your own financial affairs due to an incapacitating illness or accident. For those situations, a durable power of attorney for financial affairs has been developed to allow you to give authority to another person to take care of your financial affairs. *Durable* refers to the fact that the authority that you give to another will be in effect even if you are incapacitated. Such a document provides another person that you appoint with the same powers and authority that you, yourself, have over your property. Your appointed person can sign checks, pay bills, sign contracts, and handle all of your affairs on your behalf. In general, there are two types of durable unlimited powers of attorney for financial affairs: one that is immediately in effect and that will *remain* in effect in the event of your incapacitation, and another that *only* goes into effect if you become incapacitated. Note that this form is not contained in any of the advance health care directives that are provided on the enclosed CD. You will need to prepare this form separately if desired. For information on preparing a durable unlimited power of attorney for financial affairs, please see Chapters 6 or 9.

The combination of these five forms provides a comprehensive method by which you may provide, in advance, for a situation in which you may be unable to communicate your desires to your family, your friends, and your health care providers. It is an opportunity to carefully plan how you would like various medical situations to be handled should they arise.

You may choose to complete an entire comprehensive advance health care directive or you may simply wish to prepare a separate durable health care power of attorney, and/or a separate durable unlimited power of attorney for financial affairs. Either method is acceptable. Note that a separate living will form is not provided with this book. If you would like to prepare a living will, you are encouraged to use the state-specific advance health care directive for your state, which contains a state-specific living will form as part of that document. This will allow the provisions in your living will and the provisions in your health care power of attorney (both as part of your complete advance health care directive) to complement each other. It is important that these two documents be coordinated so that the actions that your health care agent may be asked to take on your behalf when you are unable to communicate are in line with your stated desires as shown in your living will. Keeping these two documents together as part of a comprehensive advance health care directive makes such coordination much more likely.

These forms are provided on the enclosed CD in two separate formats: either as PDF forms that may be filled in on your computer, but not altered, or as text forms that may be carefully altered to more closely fit your individual wishes and desires. The individual forms have been prepared to meet the minimum legal requirements in all states and are legally-valid in all states. Please see the detailed instructions in Chapter 1 concerning how to complete either the PDF or text versions of these individual forms, If you choose to complete the separate individual forms, please see Chapter 6 for durable unlimited power of attorney for financial affairs forms, and Chapters 7 for durable health care power of attorney forms.

When You Should Use an Advance Health Care Directive

A *'state-specific advance health care directive'* is a form that has been taken directly from the laws of your particular state. The legal effects of the language in such a document have been approved by the legislature of the state. This provides an advantage in that the legal language in such a 'statutory' form is generally familiar to health care providers in the particular state and they know that such language has been approved. This does not mean, however, that other 'non-statutory' forms are not legally valid in the state as well. Anyone may use a 'non-statutory' legal form with language that they find appropriate to their own situation, as long as the document meets certain minimum legal standards for a particular state.

You need not necessarily adopt all four sections of the document for your own use. You may select and complete any or all of the four separate sections of the form. For example, if you choose not to select a health care agent, you may use the other three parts of the form and not complete that section. Instructions for filling in the forms are contained later in this chapter. Many people find using a single comprehensive document easier than completing each separate form as an individual document. This method also provides a simple compact package that contains your entire advance health care directive with forms using legal language that most health care providers in your state are familiar with. In a few states, the legislatures have not developed specific language for one or more of the forms. These few instances are noted under the state's heading in the appendix of this book. In addition, in such situations, an appropriate and legally-valid form has been added to the directives for those states. Any such forms have been prepared following any guidelines set out by the state's legislature.

Important Note: The state-specific advance health care directive forms *do not* contain a durable unlimited power of attorney for financial affairs. As this form is not directly related to health care decision issues, it is left as a separate form located in Chapter 6. Should you desire to use this type of document to authorize someone to handle your financial affairs in the event of your disability or incapacitation, you should use one of the forms provided in Chapter 6.

Witness and Notary Requirements

All states have provided protections to ensure the validity of the advance health care directive. They have also provided legal protections against persons using undue influence to force or coerce someone into signing an advance health care directive. There are various requirements regarding who may be a witness to your signing of your advance health care directive. In general, these protections are for the purpose of ensuring that the witnesses have no actual or indirect stake in your death. These witnesses should have no connection with you from a health care or beneficiary standpoint. In most states, the witnesses must:

- Not be under 18 years of age (19 in Alabama)
- Not be related to you in any manner either by blood, marriage, or adoption
- Not be your attending physician
- Not be a patient or employee of your attending physician
- Not be a patient, physician, or employee of the health care facility in which you may be a patient
- Not be entitled to any portion of your estate upon your death under any laws of intestate succession, nor under your will or any codicil
- Not have a claim against any portion of your estate upon your death
- Not be directly financially responsible for your medical care
- Not have signed the advance health care directive for you, even at your direction
- Not be paid a fee for acting as a witness

In addition, please note that several states and the District of Columbia (Washington D.C.) have laws in effect regarding witnesses when the *declarant* (the person signing the advance health care directive) is a patient in a nursing home, boarding facility, hospital, or skilled or intermediate health care facility. In those situations, it is advisable to have a patient ombudsman, patient advocate, or the director of the health care facility act as the third witness to the signing of an advance health care directive.

These restrictions on who may be a witness to your signing of an advance health care directive require, in most cases, that the witnesses either be 1) friends who will receive nothing from you under your will, or 2) strangers. Please review the requirements for your own state in the witness statements on your particular state's form.

In addition, all of the forms included in this book, including all of the advance health care directives, are designed to be notarized. This is a requirement in most states for most forms and has been made mandatory on all of the forms in this book. The purpose of notarization in this instance is to add another level of protection against coercion or undue pressure being exerted to force anyone to sign any of these legal forms against their wishes. Sadly, such undue pressure has been applied in some cases to force senior citizens to sign legal documents against their own wishes. The requirement that one sign a document in front of a notary and in front of two additional witnesses can significantly lessen the opportunity for such abuse.

Instructions for Your Advance Health Care Directive

① Select the appropriate form from the CD. Carefully read through each section of your Advance Health Care Directive. You may wish to make two copies of the form(s) that you choose. This will allow you to use one form as a draft copy and the other form for a final copy that you, your witnesses , and a notary will sign.

② You will need to initial your choices in the first section of the form as to which sections of the entire Advance health care directive you wish to be effective. The choices are:

- Living will
- Selection of health care agent
- Designation of primary physician
- Organ donation

Please note that you may choose to exclude any of the above portions of your form and the remaining portions will be valid. If you wish to exclude one or more portions, DO NOT place your initials in the space before the section that you wish to exclude. Be careful so that you are certain you are expressing your desires exactly as you wish on these very important matters. If you do not wish to use a particular main section of the entire form, cross out that section of the form clearly and do not initial that section in either the first paragraph of the Directive or in the paragraph directly before your signature near the end of the Directive. If you do not wish to use a particular paragraph within one of the four main sections of the form, cross out that paragraph also.

Make the appropriate choices in each section where indicated by initialing the designated place or filling in the appropriate information. Depending on which form that you use, you may have many choices to initial or you may have no choices to initial. Please carefully read through the paragraphs and clauses that require choices to be certain that you understand the choices that you will be making. If you wish to add additional instructions or limitations in the places indicated on the form, please type or clearly print your instructions. If you need to add additional pages, please use the form titled "Additional Information for Advance Health Care Directive" which is also provided on the CD. If you need and use additional pages, be certain that you initial and date each added page and that you clearly label each additional page regarding which paragraph or section of the form to which it pertains.

③ In the form or section on organ donations, you may choose to either donate all of your organs or limit your donation to certain specific organs. Likewise, you may provide that the organs be used for any purpose or you may limit their use to certain purposes.

④ finally, you will need to complete the signature and witness/notary sections of your forms. When you have a completed original with no erasures or corrections, staple all of the pages together in the upper left-hand corner. Do not sign this document or fill in the date yet. You should now assemble your witnesses and a notary public to witness your signature. Be certain that your witnesses meet your specific state requirements. In addition, please note that several states and the District of Columbia have laws in effect regarding witnesses when the declarant is a patient in a nursing home, boarding facility, hospital, or skilled or intermediate health care facility. In those situations, it is advisable to have a patient ombudsman, patient advocate, or the director of the health care facility to act as the third witness to the signing of an advance health care directive. In order that your advance health care directive be accepted by all legal and medical authorities with as little difficulty as possible, it is highly recommended that you have your signing of this important document witnessed by both your appropriate witnesses and a notary public.

⑤ in front of all of the witnesses and the notary public, the following should take place in the order shown:

(a) There is no requirement that the witnesses know any of the terms of your advance health care directive or other legal forms, or that they read any of your advance health care directive or legal forms. All that is necessary is that they observe you sign your advance health care directive and that they also sign the advance health care directive as witnesses in each other's presence.

(b) You will sign your legal form at the end where indicated, exactly as your name is written on the form, in ink using a pen. At this time, if you are using a state-specific form, you should also again initial your choices as to which sections you have chosen (directly before your signature space). You will also need to fill in the date on the first page of the directive or form, date and initial each additional information page (if you have used any), and fill in your address after your signature. Once you have signed and completed all of the necessary information, pass your advance health care directive or other legal form to the first witness, who should sign and date the acknowledgment where indicated and also print his or her name.

(c) After the first witness has signed, have the advance health care directive or other legal form passed to the second witness, who should also sign and date the acknowledgment where indicated and print his or her name.

(d) Throughout this ceremony, you and all of the witnesses must remain together. The final step is for the notary public to sign in the space where indicated and complete the notarization block on the form.

(e) If you have chosen individuals to act as your health care agent (durable power of attorney for health care), you should have them sign the form at the end where shown acknowledging that they accept their appointment.

⑥ When this step is completed, your advance health care directive or individual legal form that you have signed is a valid legal document. Have several photo-copies made and, if appropriate, deliver a copy to your attending physician to have placed in your medical records file. You should also provide a copy to any person who was selected as either your health care agent or your agent for financial affairs. You may also desire to give a copy to the person you have chosen as the executor of your will, your clergy, and your spouse or other trusted relative.

If you need to add additional pages to your advance health care directive, please use the form titled "Additional Information for Advance Health Care Directive" at the end of this chapter. If you need and use additional pages, be certain that you initial and date each added page and that you clearly label each additional page regarding which paragraph or section of the form to which it pertains. You should also note in the form itself that you are using additional pages by printing or writing "See attached additional page which is incorporated by reference" in the section of the form where you wish to insert additional instructions or information.

Revoking Your Advance Health Care Directive

All states have provided methods for the easy revocation of advance health care directives and the forms that they contain. Since such forms provide authority to medical personnel to withhold life-support technology that will likely result in death to the patient, great care must be taken to insure that a change of mind by the patient is heeded. Any one of the following methods of revocation is generally acceptable:

- Physical destruction of the advance health care directive, such as tearing, burning, or mutilating the document.

- A written revocation of the advance health care directive by you or by a person acting at your direction. A form for this is provided later in this chapter and on the CD.

- An oral revocation in the presence of a witness who signs and dates an affidavit confirming a revocation. This oral declaration may take place in any manner (verbal or non-verbal). Most states allow for a person to revoke such a document by any indication (even non-verbal) of the intent to revoke an advance health care directive, regardless of his or her physical or mental condition. A form for this effect is included later in this chapter and on the CD, titled "Witness Affidavit of Oral Revocation of Advance Health Care Directive."

If your revoke your advance health care directive, make sure that you provide a copy (or notice) of this revocation to anyone or any health care facility that has a copy or original of the advance health care directive that you are revoking.

Instructions for Revocation of Advance Health Care Directive

To complete this document, fill in the following information:

① Name of person who originally signed the advance health care directive (principal or declarant)
② Date of original advance health care directive
③ State in which original advance health care directive was signed
④ Signature of person revoking advance health care directive
⑤ Date of revocation of advance health care directive

Revocation of Advance Health Care Directive

① I, _____ , am the maker and signatory of an Advance Health Care Directive which was dated ② _____ , and which was executed by me for use in the State of ③_____ .

By this written revocation, I hereby entirely revoke such Advance Health Care Directive, any Living Will, any Durable Power of Attorney for Health Care, any Organ Donation, or any other appointment or designation of a person to make any health care decisions on my behalf. I intend that all of the above mentioned documents have no force or effect whatsoever.

BY SIGNING HERE I INDICATE THAT I UNDERSTAND THE PURPOSE AND EFFECT OF THIS DOCUMENT.

④ Signature _____   ⑤ Date _____

Instructions for Witness Affidavit of Oral Revocation of Advance Health Care Directive

If it is necessary to use the Witness Affidavit of Oral Revocation of Advance Health Care Directive form, the witness should actually observe your indication of an intention to revoke your Advance Health Care Directive. This may take the form of any verbal or non-verbal direction, as long as your intent to revoke is clearly and unmistakably evident to the witness. This form does not need to be notarized to be effective. Make sure that you provide a copy of this revocation to anyone or any health care facility that has a copy or original of the Advance Health Care Directive that you are revoking.

To complete this document, fill in the following information:

1. Name of person who originally signed the advance health care directive (principal or declarant)
2. Date of original advance health care directive
3. State in which original advance health care directive was signed
4. Printed name of witness
5. Date of act of revocation
6. Signature of witness to the oral or non-verbal revoking of advance health care directive
7. Date of witness signature
8. Printed name of witness

Witness Affidavit of Oral Revocation of Advance Health Care Directive

The following person, ① _____ , herein referred to as the declarant, was the maker and signatory of an Advance Health Care Directive which was dated ② _____ , and which was executed by him or her for use in the State of ③ _____ .

By this written affidavit, I, ④ _____ , the witness, hereby affirm that on the date of ⑤ _____ , I personally witnessed the above-named declarant make known to me, through verbal and/or non-verbal methods, their clear and unmistakable intent to entirely revoke such Advance Health Care Directive, any Living Will, any Durable Power of Attorney for Health Care, any Organ Donation, or any other appointment or designation of a person to make any health care decisions on his or her behalf. It is my belief that the above-named declarant fully intended that all of the above-mentioned documents no longer have any force or effect whatsoever.

Witness Acknowledgment

The declarant is personally known to me and I believe him or her to be of sound mind and under no duress, fraud, or undue influence.

Witness Signature ⑥ _____ Date ⑦ _____

Printed Name of Witness ⑧ _____

Instructions for Additional Information for Advance Health Care Directives

If you need to add additional pages to your advance health care directive document, please use the form titled "Additional Information for Advance Health Care Directive" which is provided on the following page and on the CD. If you need to use additional pages, be certain that you initial and date each added page and that you clearly label each additional page regarding which paragraph or section of the form to which it pertains. You should also note in the form itself that you are using additional pages by printing or writing "See attached additional information page, which is incorporated by reference" in the section of the form where you wish to insert additional instructions or information. Note that this form should be attached to the original advance health care directive document prior to the signing and notarization of the original document.

To complete this document, fill in the following information:

1. Date of original advance health care directive
2. Name and address of person who originally signed advance health care directive (declarant)
3. Detailed statement of any additional information or instructions in advance health care directive (Be certain that you note the paragraph or section of the original advance health care directive where the additional information or instructions will apply).
4. Initials of declarant and date of advance health care directive

Additional Information for Advance Health Care Directive

The following information is incorporated by reference and is to be considered as a part of the Advance Health Care Directive, dated ① _____,
which was signed by the following declarant ② _____,

Declarant must initial and date at bottom of form and insert additional information here: ③

④ Initials of Declarant _____   Date _____

Appendix: State Laws Relating to Powers of Attorney

This Appendix contains a summary of the laws relating to power of attorney issues for all states and the District of Columbia (Washington D.C.). It has been compiled directly from the most recently-available statutes and has been abridged for clarity and succinctness. It is recommended that you review the listing that pertains to your home state. As you review your state's particular laws, keep in mind that your power of attorney documents are going to be interpreted under the laws of the state where you reside at the time you prepare your documents. Every effort has been made to ensure that the information contained in this Appendix is as complete and up-to-date as possible. However, state laws are subject to constant change. While most laws relating to powers of attorney are relatively stable, it is advisable to check your particular state statutes to be certain there have been no major modifications since this book was prepared, especially for those legal points that are particularly important in your situation. To simplify this process as much as possible, the exact name of the statute and the chapter or section number of where the information can be found is noted after each section of information. Any of these official statute books should be available at any public library or on the internet. A librarian will be glad to assist you in locating the correct book and in finding the appropriate pages. The correct terminology for each state is used in these listings. However, some states use certain language interchangeably. In those states, the most commonly-used language is stated. The state-by-state listings following in this Appendix contain the following information for each state:

State Website: This listing provides the internet website address of the location of the state's statutes. The addresses were current at the time of this book's publication; however, like most websites, the page addresses are subject to change. If an expired state webpage is not automatically redirected to a new site, laws can be searched at http://www.findlaw.com

State Law Description: This is the title where most of the relevant state laws on powers of attorney are contained.

Advance Health Care Directive Form: Under this listing, the exact location of a state's official Advance Health Care Directive Form is shown, if the state provides one.

Health Care Power of Attorney: The existence and location of official state health care powers of attorney are indicated in this listing.

Durable Financial Power of Attorney: This listing indicates the requirements of state law regarding durable powers of attorney for financial affairs. If the state provides the form, this is also noted.

Alabama

State Website: www.legislature.state.al.us/CodeofAlabama/1975/coatoc.htm

State Law Reference: Code of Alabama.

Advance Health Care Directive: Referred to as a Living Will (Section 22-8A-4).

Health Care Power of Attorney: State specific form is part of Advance Health Care Directive. See Chapter 10 for instructions for form on CD. (Section 22-8A-4).

Durable Financial Power of Attorney: No state-specific form. See Chapter 6 for form. (Section 26-1-2).

Arizona

State Website: www.azleg.state.az.us/

State Law Reference: Arizona Revised Statutes.

Advance Health Care Directive: Referred to as a Living Will (Sections 36-3261 and 36-3262).

Health Care Power of Attorney: State specific form is part of Advance Health Care Directive. See Chapter 10 for instructions for form on CD. (Sections 36-3221 through 36-3224).

Durable Financial Power of Attorney: State specific form. See Chapter 9. (Section 14-5501).

Alaska

State Website: www.legis.state.ak.us/folhome.htm

State Law Reference: Alaska Statutes.

Advance Health Care Directive: (Section 13.52.300).

Health Care Power of Attorney: State specific form is part of Advance Health Care Directive. See Chapter 10 for instructions for form on CD. (Section 13.52.300).

Durable Financial Power of Attorney: State specific form. See Chapter 9. (Sections 13.26.332 to 13.26.353).

Arkansas

State Website: http://www.arkleg.state.ar.us/

State Law Reference: Arkansas Code.

Advance Health Care Directive: Referred to as a Declaration. (Section 20-17-202).

Health Care Power of Attorney: No state specific form. See Chapter 7 for form. Also may use Advance Health Care Directive. See Chapter 10 for instructions for form on CD. (Section 20-13-104).

Durable Financial Power of Attorney: State specific form. See Chapter 9. (Section 28-68-402).

California

State Website: www.leginfo.ca.gov/
State Law Reference: California Law.
Advance Health Care Directive: (Probate Code, Section 4701).
Health Care Power of Attorney: State specific form is part of Advance Health Care Directive. See Chapter 10 for instructions for form on CD. (Probate Code, Section 4701).
Durable Financial Power of Attorney: State specific form. See Chapter 9. (Probate Code, Sections 4120+).

Connecticut

State Website: www.cga.state.ct.us/2001/pub/Titles.htm
State Law Reference: General Statutes of Connecticut.
Advance Health Care Directive: Referred to as Connecticut Health Care Instructions (Section 19a-575).
Health Care Power of Attorney: State specific form is part of Advance Health Care Directive. See Chapter 10 for instructions for form on CD. (Section 19a-575).
Durable Financial Power of Attorney: State specific form. See Chapter 9. (Section 45a-562).

Colorado

State Website: www.leg.state.co.us/
State Law Reference: Colorado Revised Statutes.
Advance Health Care Directive: Referred to as a Declaration as to Medical or Surgical Treatment. (Section 15-18-104).
Health Care Power of Attorney: State specific form is part of Advance Health Care Directive. See Chapter 10 for instructions for form on CD. (Section 15-14-506).
Durable Financial Power of Attorney: State specific form. See Chapter 9. (Sections 15-14-501+, 15-1-1301+, and 15-14-601+).

Delaware

State Website: http://delcode.delaware.gov/index.shtml
State Law Reference: Delaware Code.
Advance Health Care Directive: Referred to as Instructions for Health Care (Section 16-2503).
Health Care Power of Attorney: State specific form is part of Advance Health Care Directive. See Chapter 10 for instructions for form on CD. (Section 16-2503).
Durable Financial Power of Attorney: No state-specific form. See Chapter 6 for form. (Sections 12-4901+).

District of Columbia (Washington D.C.)

State Website: http://government.westlaw.com/linkedslice/default.asp?SP=DCC-1000

State Law Reference: District of Columbia Code.

Advance Health Care Directive: Referred to as a Declaration (Section 7-622).

Health Care Power of Attorney: State specific form is part of Advance Health Care Directive. See Chapter 10 for instructions for form on CD. (Section 21-2207).

Durable Financial Power of Attorney: State specific form. See Chapter 9. (Section 21-2081).

Georgia

State Website: www.legis.state.ga.us

State Law Reference: Georgia Code.

Advance Health Care Directive: Referred to as Georgia Advance Directive for Health Care (Section 31-32-4).

Health Care Power of Attorney: State specific form is part of Advance Health Care Directive. See Chapter 10 for instructions for form on CD. (Section 31-32-4).

Durable Financial Power of Attorney: State specific form. See Chapter 9. (Sections 10-6-140 through 10-6-142).

Florida

State Website: http://www.flsenate.gov/statutes/index.cfm

State Law Reference: Florida Statutes.

Advance Health Care Directive: Referred to as a Living Will (Section 765.303).

Health Care Power of Attorney: State specific form is part of Advance Health Care Directive. See Chapter 10 for instructions for form on CD. (Section 765.203).

Durable Financial Power of Attorney: No state-specific form. See Chapter 6 for form. (Section 709.08).

Hawaii

State Website: http://www.capitol.hawaii.gov/

State Law Reference: Hawaii Revised Statutes.

Advance Health Care Directive: Referred to as Instruction for Health Care (Section 327E-3).

Health Care Power of Attorney: State specific form is part of Advance Health Care Directive. See Chapter 10 for instructions for form on CD. (Section 327E3).

Durable Financial Power of Attorney: No state-specific form. See Chapter 6 for form. (Sections 551D-1 through 551D-7).

Idaho

State Website: http://www3.state.id.us/
State Law Reference: Idaho Statutes.
Advance Health Care Directive: Referred to as Idaho Living Will (Section 39-4510).
Health Care Power of Attorney: State specific form is part of Advance Health Care Directive. See Chapter 10 for instructions for form on CD. (Section 39-4510).
Durable Financial Power of Attorney: No state-specific form. See Chapter 6 for form. (Section 15-5-501+).

Indiana

State Website: http://www.in.gov/legislative/ic/code/
State Law Reference: Indiana Code.
Advance Health Care Directive: Referred to as Indiana Living Will Declaration (Section 16-36-4-10).
Health Care Power of Attorney: State specific form is part of Advance Health Care Directive. See Chapter 10 for instructions for form on CD. (Section 16-36-4-10). .
Durable Financial Power of Attorney: No state-specific form. See Chapter 6 for form. (Section 29-3-5).

Illinois

State Website: http://www.ilga.gov/
State Law Reference: Illinois Compiled Statutes.
Advance Health Care Directive: Referred to as Illinois Declaration (755 ILCS 35/3).
Health Care Power of Attorney: State specific form is part of Advance Health Care Directive. See Chapter 10 for instructions for form on CD. (755 ILCS 45/4-1+).
Durable Financial Power of Attorney: State specific form. See Chapter 9. (755 ILCS 45/2-1+).

Iowa

State Website: http://www.legis.state.ia.us/
State Law Reference: Iowa Code.
Advance Health Care Directive: Referred to as Iowa Declaration (Section 144A.3).
Health Care Power of Attorney: State specific form is part of Advance Health Care Directive. See Chapter 10 for instructions for form on CD. (Section 144B.2).
Durable Financial Power of Attorney: No state-specific form. See Chapter 6 for form. (Section 633B.1+).

Kansas

State Website: http://www.kslegislature.org/
State Law Reference: Kansas Statutes.
Advance Health Care Directive: Referred to as Kansas Declaration (Section 65-28,103).
Health Care Power of Attorney: State specific form is part of Advance Health Care Directive. See Chapter 10 for instructions for form on CD. (Section 58-629).
Durable Financial Power of Attorney: No state-specific form. See Chapter 6 for form. (Section 58-629).

Louisiana

State Website: http://www.legis.state.la.us/
State Law Reference: Louisiana Revised Statutes and Louisiana Civil Code.
Advance Health Care Directive: Referred to as Louisiana Declaration (Revised Statutes, Section 40:1299.58.3).
Health Care Power of Attorney: No state specific form. See Chapter 7 for form. Also may use Advance Health Care Directive. See Chapter 10 for instructions for form on CD. (Revised Statutes, Section 40:1299.53)
Durable Financial Power of Attorney: No state-specific form. See Chapter 6 for form. (Louisiana Civil Code 3026).

Kentucky

State Website: http://lrc.ky.gov/
State Law Reference: Kentucky Revised Statutes.
Court with Probate Jurisdiction: District Court. (Section 24A.120).
Advance Health Care Directive: Referred to as Living Will Directive (Section 311.625).
Health Care Power of Attorney: State specific form is part of Advance Health Care Directive. See Chapter 10 for instructions for form on CD. (Section 311.625)
Durable Financial Power of Attorney: No state-specific form. See Chapter 6 for form. (Section 386.093).

Maine

State Website: http://janus.state.me.us/legis/statutes/
State Law Reference: Maine Revised Statutes.
Advance Health Care Directive: Referred to as Instructions for Health Care (Section 18A-5-801).
Health Care Power of Attorney: State specific form is part of Advance Health Care Directive. See Chapter 10 for instructions for form on CD. (Section 18A-5-506). .
Durable Financial Power of Attorney: No state-specific form. See Chapter 6 for form. (Section 18A-5-508)

Maryland

State Website: http://mlis.state.md.us/

State Law Reference: Maryland Code.

Advance Health Care Directive: Referred to as Maryland Advance Directive: Planning for Future Health Care Decisions (Health General, Section 5-603).

Health Care Power of Attorney: State specific form is part of Advance Health Care Directive. See Chapter 10 for instructions for form on CD. (Health General, Section 5-603).

Durable Financial Power of Attorney: No state-specific form. See Chapter 6 for form. (Estates and Trusts, Section 13-601).

Michigan

State Website: http://www.michiganlegislature.org/

State Law Reference: Michigan Compiled Laws.

Advance Health Care Directive: No state statute. Form provided on CD.

Health Care Power of Attorney: No state specific form. See Chapter 7 for form. Also may use Advance Health Care Directive. See Chapter 10 for instructions for form on CD. (Sections 700.5506+).

Durable Financial Power of Attorney: No state-specific form. See Chapter 6 for form. (Sections 700.5501+).

Massachusetts

State Website: http://www.mass.gov/legis/laws/mgl/

State Law Reference: General Laws of Massachusetts.

Advance Health Care Directive: No state statute. Form provided on CD.

Health Care Power of Attorney: No state specific form. See Chapter 7 for form. Also may use Advance Health Care Directive. See Chapter 10 for instructions for form on CD. (Chapter 201D, Sections 1-17)

Durable Financial Power of Attorney: No state-specific form. See Chapter 6 for form. (Chapter 201B, Section 1)

Minnesota

State Website: http://www.revisor.leg.state.mn.us/stats/

State Law Reference: Minnesota Statutes.

Advance Health Care Directive: Referred to as Health Care Living Will (Section 145B.04).

Health Care Power of Attorney: State specific form is part of Advance Health Care Directive. See Chapter 10 for instructions for form on CD. (Section 145B.04).

Durable Financial Power of Attorney: No state-specific form. See Chapter 6 for form. (Section 523.07).

Mississippi

State Website: http://www.mscode.com/
State Law Reference: Mississippi Code.
Advance Health Care Directive: (Section 41-41-209).
Health Care Power of Attorney: State specific form is part of Advance Health Care Directive. See Chapter 10 for instructions for form on CD. (Section 41-41-209).
Durable Financial Power of Attorney: No state-specific form. See Chapter 6 for form. (Sections 87-3-105)

Montana

State Website: http://data.opi.state.mt.us/bills/mca_toc/index.htm
State Law Reference: Montana Code Annotated.
Advance Health Care Directive: Referred to as Montana Declaration (Section 50-9-103).
Health Care Power of Attorney: State specific form is part of Advance Health Care Directive. See Chapter 10 for instructions for form on CD. (Section 50-9-103)
Durable Financial Power of Attorney: State specific form. See Chapter 9. (Section 72-5-201).

Missouri

State Website: http://www.moga.state.mo.us/STATUTES/STATUTES.HTM#T
State Law Reference: Missouri Revised Statutes.
Advance Health Care Directive: Referred to as Missouri Declaration (Section 459.015).
Health Care Power of Attorney: No state specific form. See Chapter 7 for form. Also may use Advance Health Care Directive. See Chapter 10 for instructions for form on CD. (Section 404.822).
Durable Financial Power of Attorney: No state-specific form. See Chapter 6 for form. (Section 404.705).

Nebraska

State Website: http://www.unicam.state.ne.us/web/public/home
State Law Reference: Nebraska Revised Statutes.
Advance Health Care Directive: Referred to as Nebraska Declaration (Section 20-404).
Health Care Power of Attorney: State specific form is part of Advance Health Care Directive. See Chapter 10 for instructions for form on CD. (Section 30-3408).
Durable Financial Power of Attorney: State specific form. See Chapter 9. (Section 49-1522)

Nevada

State Website: http://www.leg.state.nv.us/NRS/

State Law Reference: Nevada Revised Statutes.

Advance Health Care Directive: Referred to as Nevada Declaration (Section 449.610).

Health Care Power of Attorney: State specific form is part of Advance Health Care Directive. See Chapter 10 for instructions for form on CD. (Section 449.830).

Durable Financial Power of Attorney: No state-specific form. See Chapter 6 for form. (Section 111.460).

New Jersey

State Website: http:/www.njleg.state.nj.us

State Law Reference: New Jersey Permanent Statutes.

Advance Health Care Directive: Referred to as Advance directive for health care (Section 26:2H-55).

Health Care Power of Attorney: No state specific form. See Chapter 7 for form. Also may use Advance Health Care Directive. See Chapter 10 for instructions for form on CD. (Section 26:2H-56).

Durable Financial Power of Attorney: No state-specific form. See Chapter 6 for form. (Section 46:2B-8.1).

New Hampshire

State Website: http://gencourt.state.nh.us/rsa/html/indexes/default.html

State Law Reference: New Hampshire Revised Statutes.

Advance Health Care Directive: Referred to as New Hampshire Declaration (Section 137-H:3).

Health Care Power of Attorney: No state specific form. See Chapter 7 for form. Also may use Advance Health Care Directive. See Chapter 10 for instructions for form on CD. (Chapter 137-J).

Durable Financial Power of Attorney: State specific form. See Chapter 9. (Section 506:6).

New Mexico

State Website: http://www.legis.state.nm.us/

State Law Reference: New Mexico Statutes.

Advance Health Care Directive: (Section 24-7A-4).

Health Care Power of Attorney: State specific form is part of Advance Health Care Directive. See Chapter 10 for instructions for form on CD. (Section 24-7A-4).

Durable Financial Power of Attorney: State specific form. See Chapter 9. (Sections 45-5-501+).

New York

State Website: http://assembly.state.ny.us/leg/

State Law Reference: New York Consolidated Laws.

Advance Health Care Directive: Referred to as Order Not To Resuscitate (Public Health, Sections 2960+).

Health Care Power of Attorney: State specific form is part of Advance Health Care Directive. See Chapter 10 for instructions for form on CD. (Public Health, Sections 2980+).

Durable Financial Power of Attorney: State specific form. See Chapter 9. (General Obligations, Sections 5-1501+).

North Dakota

State Website: http://www.legis.nd.gov/information/statutes/cent-code.html

State Law Reference: North Dakota Century Code.

Advance Health Care Directive: (Section 23-06.5-17).

Health Care Power of Attorney: State specific form is part of Advance Health Care Directive. See Chapter 10 for instructions for form on CD. (Section 23-06.5-17).

Durable Financial Power of Attorney: No state-specific form. See Chapter 6 for form. (Section 30.1-30).

North Carolina

State Website: http://www.ncga.state.nc.us/

State Law Reference: North Carolina General Statutes.

Advance Health Care Directive: Referred to as Declaration of a Desire for a Natural Death (Section 90-321).

Health Care Power of Attorney: State specific form is part of Advance Health Care Directive. See Chapter 10 for instructions for form on CD. (Sections 32A-25).

Durable Financial Power of Attorney: State specific form. See Chapter 9. (Section 32A-1+).

Ohio

State Website: http://codes.ohio.gov/

State Law Reference: Ohio Revised Code.

Advance Health Care Directive: (Section 2133.02 is not a statutory form, but it provides suggestions for phrasing the directive.

Health Care Power of Attorney: No state specific form. See Chapter 7 for form. Also may use Advance Health Care Directive. See Chapter 10 for instructions for form on CD. (Sections 1337.11+).

Durable Financial Power of Attorney: No state-specific form. See Chapter 6 for form. (Section 1337.09)

Oklahoma

State Website: http://www.lsb.state.ok.us/
State Law Reference: Oklahoma Statutes.
Advance Health Care Directive: (Section 63-3101.4).
Health Care Power of Attorney: State specific form is part of Advance Health Care Directive. See Chapter 10 for instructions for form on CD. (Section 63-3101.4).
Durable Financial Power of Attorney: State specific form. See Chapter 9. (Sections 15-1001+).

Pennsylvania

State Website: http://members.aol.com/StatutesPA/Index.html
State Law Reference: Pennsylvania Code.
Advance Health Care Directive: Referred to as Declaration. (Section 20-5404).
Health Care Power of Attorney: State specific form is part of Advance Health Care Directive. See Chapter 10 for instructions for form on CD. (Section 20-5404)
Durable Financial Power of Attorney: State specific form. See Chapter 9. (Section 20-5601)

Oregon

State Website: http://www.leg.state.or.us/ors/
State Law Reference: Oregon Revised Statutes.
Advance Health Care Directive: (Section 127.531).
Health Care Power of Attorney: State specific form is part of Advance Health Care Directive. See Chapter 10 for instructions for form on CD. (Section 127.531).
Durable Financial Power of Attorney: No state-specific form. See Chapter 6 for form. (Section 127.005).

Rhode Island

State Website: http://www.rilin.state.ri.us/Statutes/Statutes.html
State Law Reference: Rhode Island General Laws.
Advance Health Care Directive: Referred to as Declaration (Section 23-4.11-3).
Health Care Power of Attorney: State specific form is part of Advance Health Care Directive. See Chapter 10 for instructions for form on CD. (Sections 23-4.10+).
Durable Financial Power of Attorney: State specific form. See Chapter 9. (Sections 18-16-1+).

South Carolina

State Website: http://www.scstatehouse.net/

State Law Reference: South Carolina Code of Laws.

Advance Health Care Directive: Referred to as Declaration of a Desire for a Natural Death (Section 44-77-50).

Health Care Power of Attorney: State specific form is part of Advance Health Care Directive. See Chapter 10 for instructions for form on CD. (Section 62-5-504).

Durable Financial Power of Attorney: No state-specific form. See Chapter 6 for form. (Section 62-5-501).

Tennessee

State Website: http://www.michie.com

State Law Reference: Tennessee Code.

Advance Health Care Directive: Referred to as Living Will (Section 32-11-105).

Health Care Power of Attorney: No state specific form. See Chapter 7 for form. Also may use Advance Health Care Directive. See Chapter 10 for instructions for form on CD. (Section 34-6-201+).

Durable Financial Power of Attorney: No state-specific form. See Chapter 6 for form. (Section 34-6-101+)..

South Dakota

State Website: http://legis.state.sd.us/statutes/

State Law Reference: South Dakota Codified Laws.

Advance Health Care Directive: Referred to as Living Will Declaration (Section 34-12D-3).

Health Care Power of Attorney: No state specific form. See Chapter 7 for form. Also may use Advance Health Care Directive. See Chapter 10 for instructions for form on CD. (Sections 34-12C and 59-7-2.1).

Durable Financial Power of Attorney: No state-specific form. See Chapter 6 for form. (Section 43-30S-5-19).

Texas

State Website: www.capitol.state.tx.us

State Law Reference: Texas Statutes and Codes.

Advance Health Care Directive: Referred to as Directive to Physicians and Family or Surrogate (Health and Safety Code, Section 166.033).

Health Care Power of Attorney: State specific form is part of Advance Health Care Directive. See Chapter 10 for instructions for form on CD. (Health and Safety Code, Sections 166.151 through 166.166).

Durable Financial Power of Attorney: State specific form. See Chapter 9. (Probate Code, Sections 481+).

Utah

State Website: http://www.le.state.ut.us/
State Law Reference: Utah Code.
Advance Health Care Directive: (Section 75-2a-117).
Health Care Power of Attorney: State specific form is part of Advance Health Care Directive. See Chapter 10 for instructions for form on CD. (Section 75-2a-117) (effective 1/1/08).
Durable Financial Power of Attorney: No state-specific form. See Chapter 6 for form. (Section 75-5-501).

Virginia

State Website: http://leg1.state.va.us/
State Law Reference: Code of Virginia.
Advance Health Care Directive: Referred to as Advance Medical Directive (Section 54.1-2984).
Health Care Power of Attorney: State specific form is part of Advance Health Care Directive. See Chapter 10 for instructions for form on CD. (Section 54.1-2984)
Durable Financial Power of Attorney: No state-specific form. See Chapter 6 for form. (Section 11-9.1)

Vermont

State Website: http://www.leg.state.vt.us/statutes/statutes2.htm
State Law Reference: Vermont Statutes Annotated.
Advance Health Care Directive: (Title 18, Chapter 231).
Health Care Power of Attorney: No state specific form. See Chapter 7 for form. Also may use Advance Health Care Directive. See Chapter 10 for instructions for form on CD.
Durable Financial Power of Attorney: No state-specific form. See Chapter 6 for form. (Section 14-123-3508).

Washington

State Website: http://www.leg.wa.gov/
State Law Reference: Revised Code of Washington.
Advance Health Care Directive: (Section 70.122.030).
Health Care Power of Attorney: No state specific form. See Chapter 7 for form. Also may use Advance Health Care Directive. See Chapter 10 for instructions for form on CD. (Section 11.94.010+).
Durable Financial Power of Attorney: No state-specific form. See Chapter 6 for form. (Section 11.94.010+).

West Virginia

State Website: http://www.legis.state.wv.us/
State Law Reference: West Virginia Code.
Advance Health Care Directive: Referred to as Living Will (Section 16-30-4).
Health Care Power of Attorney: State specific form is part of Advance Health Care Directive. See Chapter 10 for instructions for form on CD. (Section 16-30-4).
Durable Financial Power of Attorney: No state-specific form. See Chapter 6 for form. (Sections 39-4-1 through 39-4-7).

Wyoming

State Website: http://legisweb.state.wy.us/
State Law Reference: Wyoming Statutes.
Advance Health Care Directive: (Section 35-22-403).
Health Care Power of Attorney: No state specific form. See Chapter 7 for form. Also may use Advance Health Care Directive. See Chapter 10 for instructions for form on CD. (Section 35-22-406).
Durable Financial Power of Attorney: No state-specific form. See Chapter 6 for form. (Section 3-5-101).

Wisconsin

State Website: http://www.legis.state.wi.us/
State Law Reference: Wisconsin Statutes.
Advance Health Care Directive: Referred to as Declaration to Physicians (Section 154.03).
Health Care Power of Attorney: No state specific form. See Chapter 7 for form. Also may use Advance Health Care Directive. See Chapter 10 for instructions for form on CD. (Section 155.05).
Durable Financial Power of Attorney: No state-specific form. See Chapter 6 for form. (Section 243.07).

Index

Nova Publishing Company

Small Business and Consumer Legal Books and Software

Law Made Simple Series

Advance Health Care Directives	ISBN 13: 978-1-892949-23-3	Book w/CD	$24.95
Estate Planning Simplified	ISBN 1-892949-10-5	Book w/CD	$34.95
Living Trusts Simplified	ISBN 0-935755-51-9	Book w/CD	$28.95
Living Wills Simplified	ISBN 0-935755-50-0	Book w/CD	$28.95
Personal Bankruptcy Simplified (4th Edition)	ISBN 1-892949-34-2	Book w/CD	$29.95
Personal Legal Forms Simplified (3rd Edition)	ISBN 0-935755-97-7	Book w/CD	$28.95
Powers of Attorney Simplified	ISBN 13: 978-1-892949-40-0	Book w/CD	$24.95

Small Business Made Simple Series

Corporation: Small Business Start-up Kit (2nd Edition)	ISBN 1-892949-06-7	Book w/CD	$29.95
Employer Legal Forms	ISBN 13: 978-1-892949-26-4	Book w/CD	$24.95
Landlord Legal Forms	ISBN 13: 978-1-892949-24-0	Book w/CD	$24.95
Limited Liability Company: Start-up Kit (2nd Ed.)	ISBN 13: 978-1-892949-37-0	Book w/CD	$29.95
Partnership: Start-up Kit (2nd Edition)	ISBN 1-892949-07-5	Book w/CD	$29.95
Real Estate Forms Simplified	ISBN 0-935755-09-1	Book w/CD	$29.95
S-Corporation: Small Business Start-up Kit (2nd Edition)	ISBN 1-892949-05-9	Book w/CD	$29.95
Small Business Accounting Simplified (4th Edition)	ISBN 1-892949-17-2	Book only	$24.95
Small Business Bookkeeping System Simplified	ISBN 0-935755-74-8	Book only	$14.95
Small Business Legal Forms Simplified (4th Edition)	ISBN 0-935755-98-5	Book w/CD	$29.95
Small Business Payroll System Simplified	ISBN 0-935755-55-1	Book only	$14.95
Sole Proprietorship: Start-up Kit (2nd Edition)	ISBN 1-892949-08-3	Book w/CD	$29.95

Legal Self-Help Series

Divorce Yourself: The National Divorce Kit (6th Edition)	ISBN 1-892949-12-1	Book w/CD	$39.95
Incorporate Now!: The National Corporation Kit (4th Ed.)	ISBN 1-892949-00-8	Book w/CD	$29.95
Prepare Your Own Will: The National Will Kit (6th Edition)	ISBN 1-892949-15-6	Book w/CD	$29.95

National Legal Kits

Simplified Divorce Kit (2nd Edition)	ISBN 1-892949-20-2	Book only	$19.95
Simplified Family Legal Forms Kit	ISBN 1-892949-18-0	Book only	$18.95
Simplified Incorporation Kit	ISBN 13: 978-1-892949-33-2	Book w/CD	$19.95
Simplified Limited Liability Company Kit	ISBN 1-892949-32-6	Book w/CD	$19.95
Simplified Living Will Kit	ISBN 1-892949-22-9	Book only	$15.95
Simplified S-Corporation Kit	ISBN 1-892949-31-8	Book w/CD	$19.95
Simplified Will Kit (3rd Edition)	ISBN 1-892949-21-0	Book w/CD	$19.95

Ordering Information

Distributed by:
National Book Network
4501 Forbes Blvd. Suite 200
Lanham MD 20706

Shipping: $4.50 for first & $.75 for additionall
Phone orders with Visa/MC: (800) 462-6420
Fax orders with Visa/MC: (800) 338-4550
Internet: www.novapublishing.com
Free shipping on all internet orders